William Golding:

Lord of the Flies

Writers and Their Works

William Golding:

Lord of the Flies

Raychel Haugrud Reiff

With thanks to Virginia Tiger, professor and chair of the English Department at Rutgers University, for her expert review of the manuscript.

Marshall Cavendish Benchmark
99 White Plains Road
Tarrytown, NY 10591
www.marshallcavendish.us

Library of Congress Cataloging-in-Publication Data

Reiff, Raychel Haugrud.
William Golding : Lord of the Flies / by Raychel Haugrud Reiff.
p. cm. — (Writers and their works)
Filmography: p.
Includes bibliographical references and index.
Summary: "A biography of writer William Golding that describes his era, his major work—Lord of the Flies—his life, and the legacy of his writing"—Provided by publisher.
ISBN 978-0-7614-4276-9
1. Golding, William, 1911-1993—Juvenile literature. 2. Golding, William, 1911-1993 Lord of the flies—Juvenile literature. 3. Novelists, English—20th century—Biography—Juvenile literature. I. Title.
PR6013.O35Z865 2009
823'.914—dc22
[B]
2008035968

Photo Research by Lindsay Aveilhe and Linda Sykes, Linda Sykes Picture Research, Inc., Hilton Head, SC

The photographs in this book are used by permission and through the courtesy of: David Hurn/Magnum Photos: cover, 2; MGM/The Kobal Collection: 11; Duravitski/Alamy: 16; nagelstock.com/Alamy: 18; Topfoto, London: 21; The Image Works: 25; The Imperial War Museum: 27; Cover from *Lord of the Flies* by William Golding, © 1954 by William Golding. Cover art and design by Ben Gibson. A Pedigree Book © 2006. Used with permission of The Penguin Group (USA), Inc.: 31; Cover from William Golding, *Pincher Martin*. Faber & Faber Ltd. 2005. © William Golding 1956: 35; CSU Archives/The Everett Collection: 41; Cover from *Rites of Passage* by William Golding. © 1980 Wiliam Golding. Cover Illustration by Paul Hogarth. Courtesy of Faber and Faber Limited. Isis Audio books, a division of the Clio Press Limited, Oxford, England: 46; Private Collection/The Bridgeman Art Library: 52; Hulton Archive/Getty Images: 55, 101; Mary Evans Picture Library/The Everett Collection: 59; Howard Sachs/Hulton Archive/Getty Images: 61; © Columbia Pictures/The Everett Collection: 66; Two Arts/CD/The Kobal Collection: 70; Photofest: 81; Castle Rock/Columbia/The Kobal Collection: 88; © 1979 by William Golding. FSG Classics (Farrar, Straus, Giroux), New York. All Rights Reserved: 98.

Publisher: Michelle Bisson
Art Director: Anahid Hamparian
Series Designer: Sonia Chagbatzanian

Printed in Malaysia
1 3 5 6 4 2

Contents

he head on the stake. It becomes the Lord of the Flies,
"Fancy thinking the Beast was something you could hunt
l! . . . You knew, didn't you? I'm part of you?" (128). Simon t
s consciousness. After he recovers he forces himself up
tain to discover the nature of the "beast" and finds the d
chutist, whom he releases. He then attempts to join the
to tell them about his discovery. Meanwhile, all the b
uding Ralph and Piggy, are in Jack's camp enjoying the
t and participating in the pig-killing dance. When Si
bles into the camp during the dance, the boys beat hi
h, thinking he is the beast. Alone in the woods next to
dy pig's head, Simon listens to the head on the stake
mes the Lord of the Flies, saying, "Fancy thinking the B
something you could hunt and kill! . . . You knew, didn't
part of you?" (128). Simon then loses consciousness. Afte
vers he forces himself up the mountain to discover the na
he "beast" and finds the dead parachutist, whom he relea
hen attempts to join the others to tell them about his
ry. Meanwhile, all the boys, including Ralph and Piggy,
ack's camp enjoying the pig feast and participating in
killing dance. When Simon stumbles into the camp during
e, the boys beat him to death, thinking he is the beast. A
he woods next to the bloody pig's head, Simon listens to
on the stake. It becomes the Lord of the Flies, say
cy thinking the Beast was something you could hunt and k
You knew, didn't you? I'm part of you?" (128). Simon then l
ciousness. After he recovers he forces himself up the m
to discover the nature of the "beast" and finds the d
chutist, whom he releases. He then attempts to join the
to tell them about his discovery. Meanwhile, all the b
uding Ralph and Piggy, are in Jack's camp enjoying the
t and participating in the pig-killing dance. When Si
bles into the camp during the dance, the boys beat hi
h, thinking he is the beast. Alone in the woods next to
dy pig's head, Simon listens to the head on the stake
mes the Lord of the Flies, saying, "Fancy thinking the B
something you could hunt and kill! . . . You knew, didn't
part of you?" (128). Simon then loses consciousness. Afte
vers he forces himself up the mountain to discover the na
he "beast" and finds the dead parachutist, whom he relea
hen attempts to join the others to tell them about his
ry. Meanwhile, all the boys, including Ralph and Piggy,

Introduction

WILLIAM GERALD GOLDING was born in Cornwall, England, in 1911. Fun-loving and mischievous, young Billy was a brilliant boy who read novels and taught himself to read Egyptian hieroglyphics before he started elementary school. When he was college age, Golding followed his parents' wishes and entered Oxford University to study the natural sciences with the aim of becoming a scientist; but, after two years, he switched to English literature, the subject he loved. World War II broke out several years later and Golding, now a teacher, joined the Royal British Navy. His war experience profoundly influenced his view of humankind, which he saw as inherently evil with great potential to do terrible deeds. When the war ended, Golding returned to teaching, a job he loathed.

Two days before his forty-third birthday in 1954, his life changed forever when *Lord of the Flies* was published. College students loved the novel, and Golding soon had a cult following. After the book's enthusiastic reception, Golding published several other novels, a collection of essays, and short stories, but none attained the popularity of his first work. Because of the income from book sales, Golding was able to quit his teaching job in 1962 and become a full-time writer.

In spite of his success, Golding was unhappy and depressed for about twenty years, from 1958 to 1979, during which time he suffered writer's block. However, in 1979 when he was fifty-eight years old, Golding revived his career, once again producing a number of novels and books of essays. He was awarded the Nobel Prize in Literature in 1983, ten years before he died.

Today, *Lord of the Flies* remains a popular novel, not only because of its exciting plot but also because of its intellectual and philosophical insights into the nature of human beings.

the head on the stake. It becomes the Lord of the Flies,
g, "Fancy thinking the Beast was something you could h
d kill! . . . You knew, didn't you? I'm part of you?" (128). Si
en loses consciousness. After he recovers he forces hims
the mountain to discover the nature of the "beast" and fi
e dead parachutist, whom he releases. He then attempts
in the others to tell them about his discovery. Meanwh
l the boys, including Ralph and Piggy, are in Jack's c
joying the pig feast and participating in the pig-kill
nce. When Simon stumbles into the camp during the da
e boys beat him to death, thinking he is the beast. Alone
e woods next to the bloody pig's head, Simon listens to
ad on the stake. It becomes the Lord of the Flies, say
ancy thinking the Beast was something you could hunt
ll! . . . You knew, didn't you? I'm part of you?" (128). Si
en loses consciousness. After he recovers he forces hims
the mountain to discover the nature of the "beast" and fi
e dead parachutist, whom he releases. He then attempts
in the others to tell them about his discovery. Meanwh
l the boys, including Ralph and Piggy, are in Jack's c
joying the pig feast and participating in the pig-kill
nce. When Simon stumbles into the camp during the da
e boys beat him to death, thinking he is the beast. Alone
e woods next to the bloody pig's head, Simon listens to
ad on the stake. It becomes the Lord of the Flies, say
ancy thinking the Beast was something you could hunt
ll! . . . You knew, didn't you? I'm part of you?" (128). Si
en loses consciousness. After he recovers he forces hims
the mountain to discover the nature of the "beast" and fi
e dead parachutist, whom he releases. He then attempts
in the others to tell them about his discovery. Meanwh
l the boys, including Ralph and Piggy, are in Jack's c
joying the pig feast and participating in the pig-kill
nce. When Simon stumbles into the camp during the da
e boys beat him to death, thinking he is the beast. Alone
e woods next to the bloody pig's head, Simon listens to
ad on the stake. It becomes the Lord of the Flies, say
ancy thinking the Beast was something you could hunt
ll! . . . You knew, didn't you? I'm part of you?" (128). Si
en loses consciousness. After he recovers he forces hims
the mountain to discover the nature of the "beast" and fi
e dead parachutist, whom he releases. He then attempts

Chapter 1

The Life of William Golding

WHILE WILLIAM GOLDING the novelist is famous, William Golding the person "remains virtually unknown" (Carey, "Preface," 13). He was a private man who publicly said little about himself, refused to permit his biography to be written during his lifetime, and did not publish his journals or letters. Critics Bernard S. Oldsey and Stanley Weintraub explain that although Golding was not a recluse, he "peers out at the world as through a bearded mask, and he has largely kept himself to himself except in his novels, which reveal the writer though perhaps not the man" (4). It might appear that the author of *Lord of the Flies* would be a rather brooding, thoughtful pessimist who, knowing the human capacity for evil, would prefer to live a solitary life. However, that is not the case.

Although Golding thought deeply about human depravity, he embraced life, declaring, "I am by nature an optimist" ("On the Crest of the Wave," 126). An energetic man with many interests, Golding was not only a writer but also an avid chess player, an actor, an archaeologist, a sailor, a gardener, and an accomplished musician who even toyed with the idea of becoming a concert pianist (Carey, "William Golding," 179). He loved adventure and took great pleasure in sailing his own boats, traveling, and, later in life, horseback riding. An intellectually curious man, he delighted in learning about a multitude of things, particularly languages, ancient cultures, and literatures. And he was very sociable. Golding was happily married to a lively, talented woman, Ann Brookfield, who shared his passion for living; he and his wife raised two children; and he had many good friends and acquaintances who enjoyed spending time with this affable, down-to-earth man, whose wit and dry sense of humor delighted them. At the same time, this complex man experienced long years of depression and self-doubt.

Boyhood Years, 1911-1919

Born on September 19, 1911, at his maternal grandmother's house at Karenza, Newquay, in Cornwall, England, William Gerald Golding, called Billy as a child, was part of a talented, loving, intellectual family. His forty-year-old mother, Mildred, was a musician and an early feminist who worked to gain women the right to vote. Golding stated that she "was a strong influence on me, and it was an extraordinary relationship really because she and I were very like each other. We even looked like each other" (Carey, "William Golding," 175).

His father, Alec Golding, also deeply influenced his novelist son. Born in 1876, the oldest son of a Quaker shoemaker who lived near Bristol, Alec Golding became a teacher, taking his first teaching job in Newquay, where he met Mildred Curnoe, the daughter of his landlady. After he was appointed science teacher at Marlborough Grammar School (grammar schools are non-prestigious schools for children of lower- and middle-class families) in Wiltshire, Alec married Mildred in January 1906. Golding describes his father as a self-sacrificing family man who was "generous, loving, saintly in his attitude to his family. He would give up anything for us gladly. He was understanding, too" ("The Ladder and the Tree," 173–174). He also felt his father was brilliant, explaining that "I have never met anybody who could do so much, was interested in so much, and who knew so much" ("The Ladder and the Tree," 168). Alec was a distinguished teacher who "wrote, illustrated, printed and bound" (Moss, 21), free of charge, every science textbook for the

H. G. WELLS ACHIEVED IMMORTALITY WHEN HE WROTE *THE TIME MACHINE*, AND MUCH IMPRESSED WILLIAM GOLDING'S FATHER, ALEC. THE YOUNGER GOLDING WOULD DEBUNK WELLS'S AND HIS FATHER'S IDEAS MANY YEARS LATER IN HIS CLASSIC NOVEL, *LORD OF THE FLIES*.

school: chemistry, geography, physics, botany, and zoology. He loved the arts and was an accomplished painter and musician, playing five instruments—violin, viola, cello, piano, and flute. A "socialist and agnostic, with a firmly rationalist outlook" (Carver, "William Golding," 383), Alec Golding raised Billy and his older son, Jose, born in October 1906, to believe in "the nineteenth-century scientific rationalism of T. H. Huxley and H. G. Wells" (Friedman, 12), a conviction that the world could be understood and mastered by humans. In "this exquisitely logical universe" ("The Ladder and the Tree," 172) there was no place for God, so Golding was raised as an agnostic.

At a very early age Golding formed a worldview different from his father's because he recognized the existence of darkness and evil around and within him. He first learned this philosophy from his mother, who, reflecting on the sinking of the *Titanic* when Billy was seven months old, confided in him when he was very young that she believed the world was "an exhilarating but risky place" (quoted in Oldsey and Weintraub, 4). As a toddler, he experienced the "risky" world, becoming aware of "innocence and evil, friendliness and indifference" (Tiger, 6) through his encounter with two different animals. In his first experience, which occurred when he was about eighteen months of age, he saw the world as a welcoming place when he imagined a white cockerel radiating "friendliness like a whole atmosphere of natural love" ("Scenes from a Life," 27). In his second experience, which occurred when he was briefly separated from his parents when they were walking in the woods one winter afternoon, he perceived the world as terrifying when he saw a dark stag's head of "stillness and terrible indifference" (34) staring at him, and he ran screaming to find his parents.

As a result of his early awareness of an indifferent or evil world, Billy became afraid of unknown or unexplainable things. His fears were fueled by his mother, who caused him to be "scared stiff of the uncanny" (Carey, "William Golding," 177) by telling him stories of dead people who had returned to earth as ghosts. It is no wonder that Billy learned "to fear and hate" ("Scenes from a Life," 26) his family's dark fourteenth-century house at 29 The Green in Marlborough and the bordering graveyard. He felt the presence of an evil, ghostlike force coming from the cemetery where he imagined "the dead lay, their heads under our wall, the rest of them projecting from their own place into our garden, their feet, their knees even, tucked under our lawn" ("The Ladder and the Tree," 167). Imagining that spirits permeated the walls of his house, the young boy was terrified of its dark cellar and did not dare be in it alone to use the swing his father had set up there. He could not talk to his parents about this evil "enemy" that "came with darkness" and "reduced [him] to a shuddering terror that was incurable because it was indescribable" (167) because "[t]hey knew so much, had such certainties" (170) that they would think he was silly. Therefore, he felt alone in a terrifying world, raised by parents who "were lovingly concerned with their son's welfare [but found] it difficult to understand him or answer his deepest needs" (Crompton, 54).

Although the young boy suffered from inner terrors, his exterior world was stable but isolated. Golding relates that before his first day of school he "had known no one outside my own family—nothing but walks with Lily [his nurse] or my parents, and long holidays by a Cornish sea" ("Billy the Kid," 159), where his maternal grandparents lived. Furthermore, he was somewhat spoiled because he "was used to being adored," in part because he was a cute little boy whom his mother described as having "eyes like cornflowers and hair like a field of ripe corn" (159).

Billy seems to have been a brilliant child who was especially interested in languages. Before he started school in 1919 he had read a number of novels, studied words (he relates that he had a "passion for words in themselves, and collected them like stamps or birds' eggs") ("Billy the Kid," 159), and taught himself to read Egyptian hieroglyphics because of his keen interest in the ancient Egyptians. This came about when he decided to write a play about ancient Egypt when he was seven, but "[h]alf way through the first page of my scrawl," he writes, "I was struck by the thought that these characters ought to speak in Ancient Egyptian, a language with which I was unacquainted at the time. I abandoned my play therefore and started to learn hieroglyphics" ("Egypt from My Inside," 71).

School Years, 1919-1934

When Billy was school-aged, neither he nor his brother were able to enroll in England's best schools, the public ones, because the family was not upper-class. In fact, Golding's father, in spite of his brilliance, "could never have taught" (Tiger, 4) at the Marlborough public school, an elite private school, but instead spent forty years "teaching the rudiments of science to the rather stolid children of local tradesmen and farmers" (Moss, 16). Golding explains that:

> "[i]n the dreadful English scheme of things at that time, . . . we had our subtle place. Those unbelievable gradations ensured that though my parents could not afford to send my brother and me to a public school, we should nevertheless go to a grammar school. Moreover we must not go first to an elementary school but to a dame school [a small private school usually run by women that provided an education for children who were not of the upper class] where the children were nicer though the education was not so good. In fact, like every boy except the very high and the very low in those days, we walked a social tightrope, could not mix with the riotous children who made such a noise and played such wonderful games on the Green." ("The Ladder and the Tree,"167–168)

Billy started dame school in 1919 when he was almost eight years old. During his early weeks at school, he demonstrated that his father was right when he wrote in his diary in 1918, "Billy is the artistic member of the family. He is a little rascal" (quoted in Carey, "William Golding," 175). At first the little boy was determined to learn only those subjects that interested him; and, therefore, he spent his time "scrawling a list of words" when he "was supposed to be writing out [his] tables, or even dividing four oranges between two poor boys," or "learning [his] Collect," a short prayer used in church for special occasions ("Billy the Kid," 159–160).

Billy showed his rascality even more clearly in his relationships with other students because he looked forward to recess when he could fight the other boys. Golding explains, "I lacked opposition, and yearned to be victorious. The legendary heroes Achilles, Lancelot and Æneas should have given me a sense of human nobility but they gave me instead a desire to be a successful bruiser" ("Billy the Kid," 159). He immediately became the schoolyard bully and found fighting "to be just as delightful as I had thought. I was chunky and zestful and enjoyed hurting people. I exulted in victory, in the complete subjugation of my adversary, and thought that they should enjoy it too—or at least be glad to suffer for my sake" (161). When Billy realized the other children did not like him, he was devastated. Through the work of his loving mother and wise teacher, the schoolgirls made Billy play with them, so he no longer had an opportunity to fight with the boys, and he soon got along with the other students. At the end of the term, he received a prize for general improvement.

After two years at dame school Golding attended Marlborough Grammar School, where he received his secondary education from 1921 through 1930. Here the "competitive and clever" and "reasonably diligent" Golding was an all-around student. He played a number of musical instruments, won awards for drawing, played sports (cricket, golf, hockey, and rugby), and was a good sprinter (Carver, "William Golding," 383–384). But reading was probably his favorite activity. He loved adult classics, such as Jonathan Swift's *Gulliver's Travels*, John Bunyan's *The Pilgrim's Progress*, and Daniel Defoe's *Robinson Crusoe*; at the same time, he was captivated by children's classics.

GOLDING WAS RAISED IN THE TOWN OF MARLBOROUGH AND ATTENDED THE LOCAL GRAMMAR SCHOOL WHERE HIS FATHER WAS A SCIENCE TEACHER.

With his love for words and novels, it is not too surprising that Golding decided to write his own novel when he was about twelve years old. It was an ambitious project; he expected to write twelve sections and include a history of the rise of trade unionism. As an adult, Golding laughed at his attempt. He recalled that his opening sentence, "I was born in the Parish of St Mawes, in the Duchy of Cornwall, in the year 1791, of rich but honest parents," made him so arrogant that he was "overcome by its wit and saw it was a standard I could not possibly maintain" ("A Moving Target," 160), so he moved on to volume two. After writing a second masterful sentence, "Proverbs are the refuge of the inarticulate," he quit writing, "defeated by my own brilliance" ("A Moving Target,"160).

One subject Golding did not want to learn was Latin, a language he needed to master in order to become a scientist, as his parents expected. In his essay "The Ladder and the Tree," Golding writes that after he got "no marks at all in a Latin test and minus one for bad writing," he and his father had a "show down" (173). He humorously tells the serious story of his "capitulation to his father's kindly admonition that he come down from mystery's figurative tree, learn his Latin, go up to Oxford, study science and so succeed" (Tiger, 7). When he finally did study Latin, not unexpectedly, given his aptitude for languages, Golding found it "ridiculously easy" ("The Ladder and the Tree," 174) and later even wrote verse in it (Carver, "William Golding," 384).

During these years, Golding led a happy and interesting home life. One of his father's admiring students wrote that the Goldings' home "must have been a wonderful environment in which to grow up" (Moss, 26). Golding's entire family was musical (like his father, Golding played five instruments—piano, cello, oboe, violin, and viola), and the family took pleasure in playing together; "people

At Oxford University, William Golding made the decision to drop the study of science in favor of literature, a choice that would change his life and the lives of millions of readers.

using the path that passed the Golding house would hear on many, many evenings the sound of quartets or sonatas floating across the churchyard" (Moss, 23). Golding and his brother, Jose, were good companions and enjoyed taking long walks together in the Wiltshire countryside. Alec kept things exciting with his knowledge and inventions. One of his most fascinating inventions was a radio that the family listened to enthusiastically every night in the 1920s and after (Carver, "William Golding," 384).

Although young Golding was determined to be a poet (Carver, "William Golding," 384), he did not immediately follow his dreams. Instead, he did what his parents desired and, after graduating from Marlborough School in 1930, entered Brasenose College, Oxford, to study natural sciences—botany, zoology, chemistry, and physics. Although he had "a great admiration" (Biles, 88) for these fields, he was not happy with his choice of study and even underwent hypnotism during his first year at the university because, he says, "I was eager for any experience that would release me from an increasingly grey daylight and from the labs where the frogs twitched and the rabbits' guts swelled in the hot summer humidity" ("My First Book," 152).

By his second year Golding seems to have realized that he had made a mistake in choosing to study science, but he continued, fearing that a switch to English literature "would hurt my father so much" (Biles, 89–90). Nevertheless, he began reading a lot of literature. At the end of that year Golding, after passing his science exam, decided to drop his scientific studies. Eileen Hogben, Golding's younger first cousin who was adopted by the Goldings at age thirteen when her parents died, "remembers that during the summer of 1932 there were intense discussions between Golding and his father. Golding wished to change to English Literature. This would involve further expense (and Golding was not a frugal student). However, Alec agreed, and, characteristically, once he had taken the decision, helped his son with his new syllabus, writing out a translation of *Beowulf* [a long poem written in Old English], for example" (Carver, "William Golding," 384). That fall Golding began studying literature, a subject he felt was much more important than science because, he explains, "Our humanity rests in the capacity to make value judgments, unscientific assessments, the power to decide that this is right, that wrong, this ugly, that beautiful, this just, that unjust. . . . They can be answered only by the methods of philosophy and the arts" ("On the Crest of the Wave," 130).

During his Oxford years, Golding, with his "life-long love of rhythm, sound, and in particular, rhyme" ("My First Book," 147), spent time writing poetry. He borrowed a friend's typewriter and "composed poetic reflections on nature, unrequited love, the call of the sea, and the seduction of rationalism" (Dick, 2). Another student, his friend Adam Bittleston, knew an editor at Macmillan and "sent a sheaf of my verses to the publisher" ("My First Book," 152). Macmillan published Golding's thirty-four page book *Poems* as part of the Contemporary Poets series in 1934. Excited, Golding "wondered how big my fan mail would be" and was extremely disappointed when "nothing happened at all. The little book was not even reviewed" ("Crosses," 27). Golding's later assessment that the poems are "poor, thin things" (27) is the general view of critics, who dismiss them as works of a young writer. For example, James Gindin declares that "the poems justify Golding's later dismissal of them as inconsequential and adolescent. A number are rather vague, vapid and generally derivative exercises in romantic feeling" (3), while Bernard F. Dick feels that as "literature, they have no great value" (2). Golding received five pounds for this book; by 1981, after he was famous, this small book was selling in the United States for four thousand dollars ("My First Book," 152, 147).

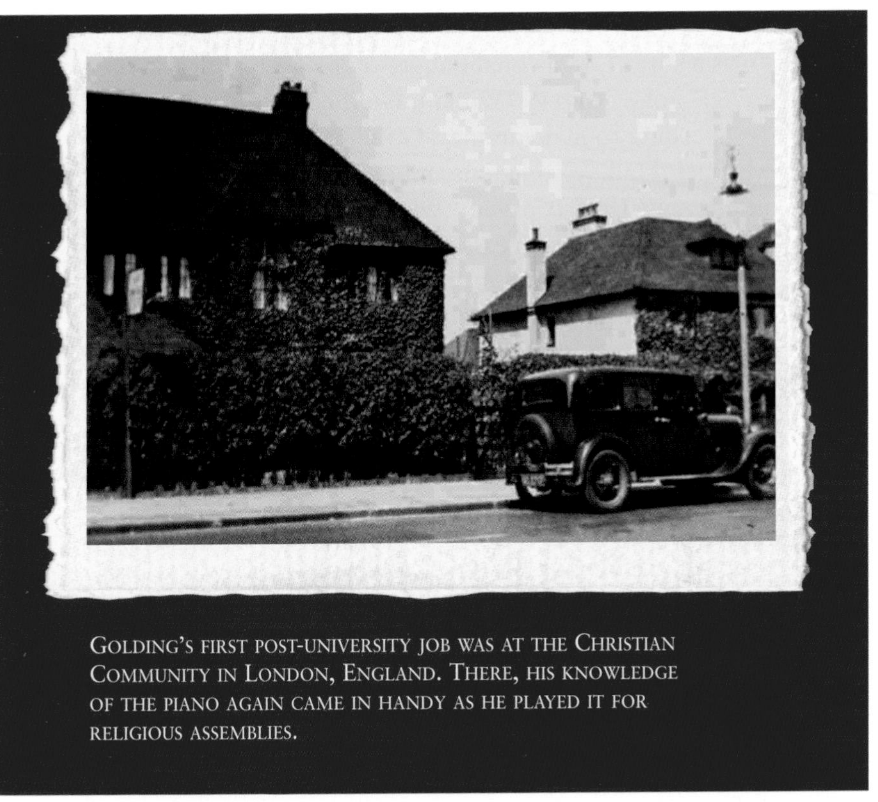

GOLDING'S FIRST POST-UNIVERSITY JOB WAS AT THE CHRISTIAN COMMUNITY IN LONDON, ENGLAND. THERE, HIS KNOWLEDGE OF THE PIANO AGAIN CAME IN HANDY AS HE PLAYED IT FOR RELIGIOUS ASSEMBLIES.

After this publication, Golding "went on writing verses . . . and got together another book" ("Crosses," 27), but he did not find a publisher.

Young Adult Years, 1934-1940

After graduating with honors from Oxford in June 1934, Golding drifted from job to job for the next five years, unclear what direction his life should take. He was involved in several creative activities. First, he lived at the Christian Community headquarters in London, where he played the piano for assemblies and wrote a play that was performed by the members of the Community. Later that year and probably also in 1935, he became a professional actor. Golding worked at the Little Theatre in Hampstead and the Citizen's Theatre in Bath, but he reports that he "was a sort of occasional hanger-on" who had "very, very trivial" roles (Carey, "William Golding," 178).

Needing to make money, Golding became a teacher at Michael Hall, a religious school in Streatham, South London, in 1935 (Carver, "William Golding," 385). Even though he spent two years there teaching a variety of subjects and participating in musical and dramatic performances, he did not like teaching; what he really wanted to do was become a writer. In the summer of 1937 he asked writer David Garnett for advice on how to make a living by writing. Even though Garnett gave him practical information, Golding decided not to pursue this career and instead went back to Oxford to study for a teaching qualification. About six months later, he spent a semester practice-teaching at Bishop Wordsworth's School, a prestigious cathedral school for children of the upper classes, in Salisbury.

Golding received his teaching diploma from Oxford in June 1938, and in September he took a job at Maidstone Grammar School in Kent, a position he obtained because the school needed a musician to teach a musically talented pupil. Here, Golding led a very active life. Besides supervising this student, he also ran a chamber choir, taught English, directed plays, and participated in school activities, including cricket, rugby, music, and drama. Outside the school, he taught at the local prison, put on a political pageant in the town, and joined a political book club. Not surprisingly, he is remembered as "quite jolly, very friendly and full of energy" (Carver, "Harbour and Voyage," 45–46).

As a result of these activities, Golding, now twenty-seven years old, met the Brookfields, a large, prominent, local family. The oldest daughter, twenty-six-year-old Ann—a chemist—was "a beauty, with blue eyes, black hair, and lovely features" who "had lovely clothes, went out to dances, acted, organized a local hockey team [and]

. . . was passionately involved in politics" (Carver, "Harbour and Voyage," 46). When they met in London during the fall of 1938 or early in 1939 at a meeting of a book club, they immediately fell in love, even though both were engaged to marry other people. Their daughter, Judy Carver, reports that "it was a *coup de foudre*. They found themselves later that evening, walking up the Strand together, talking excitedly in rapid French. From that moment on they were a couple, a partnership, each more important to the other than anyone else in the world. Other ties, with siblings, parents, friends, receded for both" (47). Although Ann's breakup with her fiancé was fairly easy, Golding's "was an ugly one and angered his parents. He felt his fiancée's misery, his parents' disappointment and displeasure, and the resultant guilt . . . recurred in thought and in terrible dreams at least as late as the 1970s. Nevertheless, he also had a contradictory feeling, of a right to freedom, to love. There was great happiness" (48). On September 30, 1939, he and Ann were married in the Maidstone Registry Office. Their marriage, which lasted more than fifty years, until death, was a very happy one. Their daughter describes them as soulmates: "They entertained each other, first and foremost. They talked. . . . And their conversation was always a brilliant, real activity, an involvement, like a journey that was full of new experience—for both. They gave each other their thoughts. They also poked fun at each other, gently for the most part. . . . They shared passions: stained glass; . . . language; gardening; conversation. They made room for each other's passions and did their best to share them." Ann even participated in Golding's love of the sea, where she "accompanied and helped him in a series of adventures which would have daunted many" (44–45).

In April 1940 the newlyweds moved into a small cottage in the Wiltshire village of Bowerchalke, near Salisbury, when Golding took a job as schoolmaster at Bishop Wordsworth's School. That September their first child, David, was born. By this time, England was involved in World War II. Like many other young, patriotic men and women of England, William Golding served his country in this war. In December 1940 he took a leave of absence from Bishop Wordsworth's School and joined the Royal Navy.

The War Years, 1941-1945

Golding spent almost the entire war in the naval service, first as an ordinary seaman and later as an officer. These years destroyed any idealism Golding may have held about the rational or beneficent nature of human beings.

His first active service was on the HMS *Galatea* and the destroyer *Orion* in the North Atlantic Ocean. Here he was involved in one of the most important naval actions of the war—the pursuit and sinking of the *Bismarck*, a powerful German battleship that was chased by every available British warship after it had sunk a British battle cruiser and damaged a British battleship. Golding's next assignment was in Liverpool, where he spent many hours on guard duty in the Gladstone Dock.

After a year of service Golding became an officer. In the spring of 1942 he was assigned to Buckinghamshire to work at a weapons research organization that was devoted to inventing and developing weapons. At first Golding enjoyed this work, telling interviewer Jack I. Biles, "I was there for very nearly a year, right in the middle of England, all dressed up as a naval officer and trying to invent things that would sink submarines. It was fantastic. I enjoyed a lot of it, made immense bangs" (26). In reality, his job was dangerous—he tested explosives. Once he nearly killed himself. As he relates, "One day I put a lot of detonators in my pocket and dropped a torch battery in with them and blew myself up" (26–27). After his recovery he asked to return to active sea duty, deciding that "if anybody is going to blow me up, it can be somebody else'" (27).

GOLDING'S FIRST ACTIVE SERVICE DURING WORLD WAR II WAS ON THE HMS *GALATEA* IN THE ATLANTIC OCEAN.

When he was reassigned to sea duty, Golding was given the job of mine sweeping. After training in Scotland, he was sent to New York in 1943 to bring a minesweeper back to England. By the time he returned home, "the mine problem had been licked, and they were all ready for invading Europe" (Biles, 27).

With his knowledge of explosives, Golding was pleased to be appointed as the commander of a rocket-launching craft that provided naval support during the invasion of France on June 6, 1944, a day forever after known as D-day. Getting to the D-day invasion location was one of the most dangerous things Golding did during the war. Golding's first lieutenant, who was on watch the night before the invasion, got lost. When Golding took over at 2:00 a.m. and realized they were miles from their assigned position, he steered his ship at full speed over mine-infested waters. (He later found out that the water labeled "mine-infested" was only a decoy to frighten the enemy.) He confesses, "I was frightened—not immediately of the mines we might set off at any moment, nor of the batteries ashore, nor the thousands of enemy aircraft we had been promised. I was frightened, of all things, of being late and jeered at" ("The English Channel," 42). Golding arrived on time and successfully bombarded the French coast with rockets so that the Nazis could not easily fire on the combined infantry as it swarmed onto the beach. Although he made light of the job, calling it "the safest job in the business" (Biles, 28), it was really a frightening and dangerous one. One critic points out that Golding "has not told of his fear of this ship, the nagging knowledge that one spark, one tracer bullet would blow up his floating fireworks factory to blazes. He has not told of the moral doubt of choosing to risk his men's lives by sailing over a minefield in order not to be mocked for arriving late for the greatest sea invasion there ever was" (Sinclair, 171–172).

In one of his final war assignments, Golding was once more in an extremely dangerous situation during the invasion of the Dutch island of Walcheren in November 1944. His ship was ordered to pass through a narrow channel without air support, a very grim situation for Golding and his crew. As he explains: "We knew that the only thing

Golding took part in the extremely dangerous invasion of Walcheren at the end of World War II. Though he survived the grim battle, the war had an enormous effect on the way that he looked at the world and the world's peoples.

that all the support craft could do . . . would be that we would have to steam up and down or in and out, looking fierce and heroic and getting sunk, while the army got ashore. I knew exactly what the situation was and I was very, very frightened" (Biles, 28). Almost all of the other rocket ships were destroyed by shells, phosphorus, and bombs. Golding "was reported missing, and the operation itself resulted in heavy casualties. But he had survived, against the odds, though many of his closest friends died. It was an episode which he recalled with particular horror, amid all the horrors of that time" (Carver, "Harbour and Voyage," 49).

After the war ended in Europe in May 1945, Golding was offered a promotion and a command in the Far East. But, wishing to return to civilian life, he turned it down. By September, the war in the Far East was over.

Golding's daughter says that her father's war experiences "affected him profoundly, both because of his own actions, and through witnessing the death or terrible injuries of his comrades. In an unpublished work written in the winter of 1947–1948, he describes seeing a companion vessel blown up and, as he says, even worse, another one mined and sinking, when he could not turn his own ship around to save the men in the stricken one. He commented, 'These are memories to dim the sunlight'" (Carver, "William Golding," 387).

The war was Golding's greatest educational experience, confirming "for him the process, begun with the sinking of the *Titanic*, of shattering the liberal and optimistic image of man" (Medcalf, *William Golding*, 6). Golding explains that as a young man, "[b]efore the second world war I believed in the perfectibility of social man: that a correct structure of society would produce good will; and that therefore you could remove all social ills by a reorganization of society" ("Fable," 86). But, after having "had one's nose rubbed in the human condition" (Biles, 33), he realized that "man was sick—not exceptional man, but average man . . . the condition of man was to be a morally diseased creation" ("Fable," 87). Unlike many of his countrymen, who complacently believed that only the Nazis were capable of great evil, Golding had "seen enough and thought enough to realize that every single one of us could be Nazis" because "what the Nazis were doing, they were doing because certain capacities in them, certain deficiencies, certain anything you like in them, had been freed, and they were just people like us, in different circumstances" (Biles, 3, 34). Throughout the rest of his life, Golding believed that all humans are born with original sin and "are about balanced between potentiality for good and potentiality for bad" (43).

Golding regarded his service in the navy as one of the two "greatest influences on his writing" (Medcalf, *William Golding*, 6). The other, learning ancient Greek, also occurred during the war years. In his free time on board ship, Golding found consolation in "reading and rereading Homer, rediscovering through the epics a sense of the continuity of human history" (Oldsey and Weintraub, 9). Golding's friend, scholar Stephen Medcalf, suggests that Golding's knowledge of the Greek language and literature helped change him from a minor poet into an original novelist (*William Golding*, 6–8), something Golding seems to agree with: "If I really had to adopt literary parentage . . . I should name thunderous great names like Euripides, and Sophocles, and perhaps even Herodotus. And I might go so far as to say that I have a profound admiration . . . for Homer" (quoted in Baker, xvii).

One additional thing happened during the war years that made a huge difference in Golding's writing career: he decided to concentrate on writing prose instead of poetry. His daughter states that in the fall of 1944, "Golding found time in his captain's cabin to write a kind of literary chronicle of progress so far, and he seems to have taken some sort of decision to move away from poetry" (Carver, "William Golding," 387).

The Post-War Years, 1945-1953

In the nine years between the end of World War II and the publication of *Lord of the Flies*, Golding returned to teaching at Bishop Wordsworth's School in Salisbury. In 1946 the Goldings—William, Ann, David, and daughter, Judith Diana, born in July 1945—moved to Salisbury and lived in an apartment owned by the city council. Golding still was not an enthusiastic teacher; in fact, he found the teaching of English "something of a chore," and students remember him in class as "rather reserved" (Barrett, 28). However, outside the classroom he enthusiastically embraced activities—running several after-school clubs, commanding the school Combined Cadet Force, acting in and directing plays, singing in the school choir, playing in the school orchestra, teaching music and literature for the Workers' Educational Association, playing chess, sailing, and raising a family (Carver, "Harbour and Voyage," 50). He was so busy that his daughter has "wondered if the post-war period was for him, at least, partly one of real depression, masked by incessant activity" (51).

By this time, Golding, enjoying the sea and loving the English coastline, had developed a keen interest in sailing. In 1947 the Goldings had saved enough money to purchase an old ship's lifeboat and convert it into a sailing vessel that they named the *Seahorse*. That summer, they took a family vacation on a sailboat. This trip provided the impetus for Golding to return to writing and, during the next winter, he wrote an unpublished account of their trip.

Once he started writing again, it became his most prominent activity. By 1952, Golding had produced "two shortish novels (unpublished and likely to remain so),"

THOUGH *LORD OF THE FLIES* GOT SOME GOOD INITIAL REVIEWS, IT WAS SOME TIME BEFORE SALES ALLOWED GOLDING TO GIVE UP HIS DAY JOB—TEACHING—AND FOCUS ON WRITING MORE FICTION.

plus "poems, published and unpublished, two accounts of holidays in [the family's] first boat *Seahorse*, and part of a diary, as well as other writing probably stemming from this period" (Carver, "Harbour and Voyage," 50). When his novels were rejected by publishers, Golding was depressed, but he soon realized that they were imitative books, "splendid examples of other people's work" (Carey, "William Golding," 189). Perceiving "the folly of writing other people's books for them," he says, "I determined to write, but for myself" ("A Moving Target," 162).

With this new resolve, Golding began to work on an original novel in the fall of 1952. He recalls how his book, which he called *Strangers from Within*, began:

> More than a quarter of a century ago I sat on one side of the fireplace and my wife on the other. We had just put the children to bed after reading to the elder some adventure story or other—Coral Island, Treasure Island, Coconut Island, Pirate Island, Magic Island, God knows what island. . . . But I was tired of these islands with their paper-cutout goodies and baddies and everything for the best in the best of all possible worlds. I said to my wife, "Wouldn't it be a good idea if I wrote a story about boys on an island and let them behave the way they really would?" She replied at once, "That's a first class idea. You write it." So I sat down and wrote it. ("A Moving Target," 162–163)

With Ann's encouragement, Golding worked hard on this novel, composing it in the rapid style that became his pattern—writing "2000 words a day until it's finished" (Carey, "William Golding," 187). Three or four months later, in January 1953, he had completed his novel. Twenty-one publishers rejected it before he sent it to Faber and Faber (Reilly, 3), where the new editor, Charles

Monteith, picked it out of the rejected pile of novels, began to read it, and was enthralled.

The Years of the First Novels, 1954-1958

On September 17, 1954, the novel, with some changes to the text and with a new title, *Lord of the Flies*, appeared in England. A year later, it was published in the United States. Tracing the evils found in society back to individuals because "man produces evil as a bee produces honey" (Golding, "Fable," 87), "*Lord of the Flies* perforated *The Coral Island*'s easy optimism" (Tiger, 8) that evil lies outside civilized beings and is found only in savages and pirates that visit the island. Golding's English schoolboys, shipwrecked on a beautiful tropical island during a war, quickly destroy it, worship an idol, and kill two boys before they are rescued by a naval officer, showing "that within us all, eagerly waiting to be let out, lie savages" (Callil and Tóibín, 66).

In spite of receiving enthusiastic reviews, *Lord of the Flies* was at first only somewhat successful commercially. But soon "it became a literary bombshell—acclaimed by the critics, its paperback selling in the millions throughout the English-speaking world" (Reilly, 3). Frank Kermode praised it as "a work of genius by a writer . . . in superbly full possession of his great powers" (213), while Lionel Trilling declared that it was "one of the most striking literary phenomena of recent years" (quoted in Page, 23).

Twelve months after *Lord of the Flies* appeared, Golding's second novel, *The Inheritors*, was published, a book he also composed in record time, writing "between two and three thousand words a day, something like that, in three weeks, three weeks plus" and then revising it once (Biles, 62). Like *Lord of the Flies*, this novel was also inspired by a book, H. G. Wells's *Outline of History*. Golding says he did not believe in Wells's idea of "some kind of social perfectibility in man" and "looked at the premises that he was using and decided I didn't agree with them. So I stood them on their heads" (4). Unlike Wells's evil, unenlightened Neanderthals who were replaced by new and better humans, Golding's primitive Neanderthals are innocent beings who are gradually exterminated by a more intelligent, but also more depraved, type of human being, the direct ancestors of present-day people. *The Inheritors*, Golding's "favourite [*sic*] among his novels" (Carver, "William Golding," 388–389), is also highly regarded by many critics who find it "perhaps the most perfect of Golding's works" (Gregor and Kinkead-Weekes, 97).

After the sales of these two successful novels, the Goldings had more money, and in 1956 they were able to buy a new boat, *Wild Rose*, which they took to France in August. The journey was a harrowing one: for three days, a strong gale raged, threatening to destroy the boat and the crew. In spite of the dangers, Golding did not lose his enthusiasm for sailing, nor his respect for the sea, which he described as "the cruelest bit of nature. Its cruelty is past believing" (Carey, "William Golding," 181).

Golding had two new works, a novel and a short story, published in 1956. Like his first two novels, *Pincher Martin*, an account of the after-death experiences of a drowned naval officer, was written quickly in three or four weeks over a Christmas holiday (Biles, 63). The plot seems to be straightforward: During World War II, Christopher Hadley (Pincher) Martin's ship is hit by a torpedo, and he is cast away on a rock in the ocean, where he survives for the next several days, becoming more and more tormented about the terrible things he did during his life. Finally, he dies, and his body drifts to an inhabited coast where it is discovered. In the last sentence of the novel, the reader learns that Martin's story of his struggle to survive on the rock is all an illusion because he had immediately died in the water. This ending has caused controversy among critics. Stephen Medcalf, greatly moved by this novel's

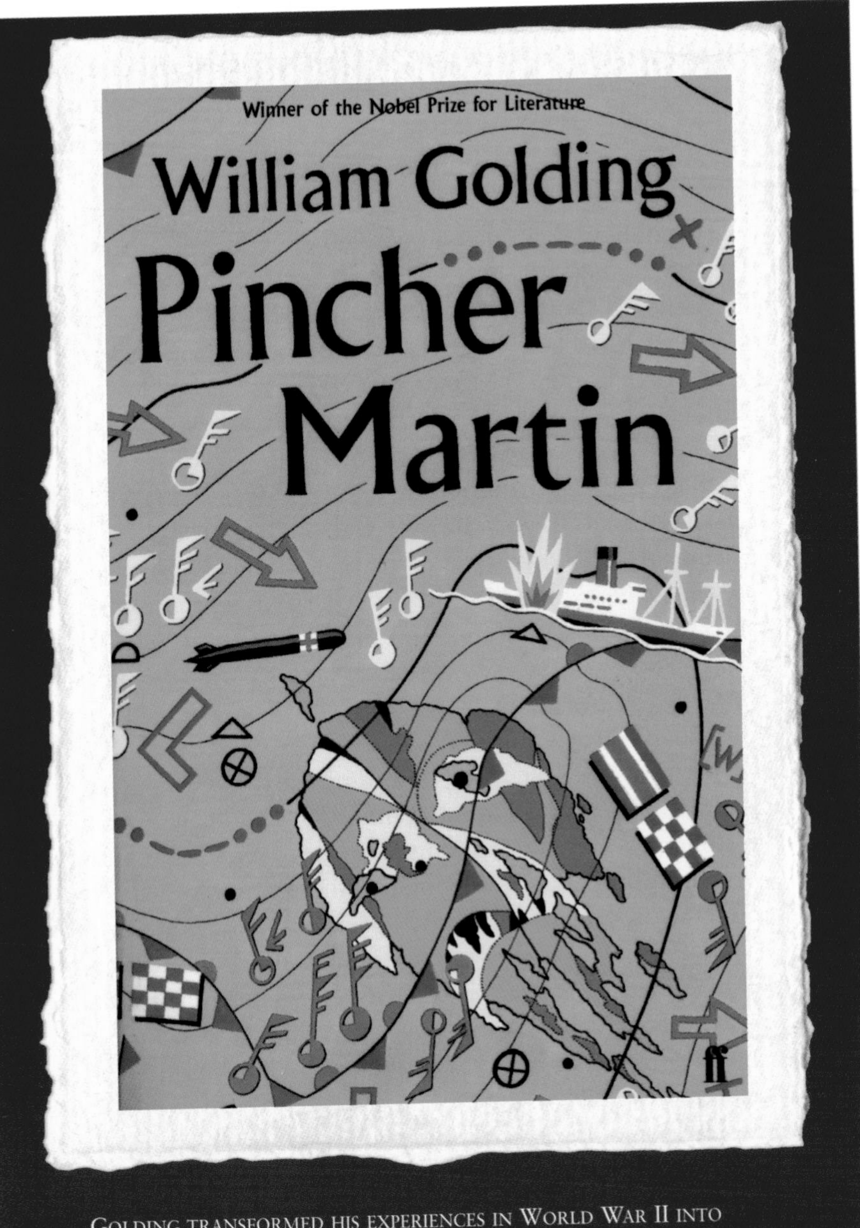

GOLDING TRANSFORMED HIS EXPERIENCES IN WORLD WAR II INTO NOVELS. *PINCHER MARTIN* TELLS THE TALE OF A NAVAL OFFICER WHO DROWNED AT SEA WHEN HIS WARSHIP IS HIT BY A TORPEDO.

conclusion, writes that "at first reading the last sentence left me trembling" (*William Golding*, 24). However, other commentators are not enthusiastic. For example, Angus Wilson remarks, "Even in *Pincher Martin*, my own doubt is how much the pay-off at the end really strengthens the novel. . . . The [novel] is so great, so considerable on its own account, that when you get to that end, you say, 'Ah, yes, I see,' and you think, 'How clever, how wonderful,' but then you think afterwards, 'Yes, but did it really add to all that I had known already?'" (quoted in Biles, 69).

Golding's other 1956 publication was the story "Envoy Extraordinary," one of three stories in *Sometime, Never: Three Tales of the Imagination*, with John Wyndham and Mervyn Peake contributing the other two. It is a science fiction tale of a Roman emperor who, having been offered a steamship, explosives, and a printing press by an inventor, saves the civilized world from the evils of industrialism, worldwide warfare, and inferior, mass-produced books. This clever story was adapted into a play, *The Brass Butterfly*, and in 1958, it was performed in England. In July the text was published.

By now Golding, who was admitted to fellowship in the Royal Society of Literature in 1955, had become part of London's literary scene. By 1957 he was able to supplement his income by writing essays, reviews, and travel reports. Although Golding did not publish a new novel in 1957, *Pincher Martin* was published in the United States with a new title, *The Two Deaths of Christopher Martin*. His headmaster was supportive of Golding's new career and gave him time off, making it possible for him to both teach and write.

His home life was also good. His family still enjoyed vacationing together on the sea in *Wild Rose*. In 1958, the Goldings were finally able to afford their own home; they moved from Salisbury to a house they bought in Bowerchalke.

The Years of Struggle, 1958-1967

In spite of his successes, by the late 1950s Golding was entering into a depressing period in his life. His daughter lists three reasons for his unhappiness. First, he was becoming worn out because of his many activities. Second, he suffered from writer's block and found it difficult to write another novel after he finished writing his fourth book, *Free Fall*, in 1958 or early 1959; in the nine years from 1958 to 1967, Golding wrote only two more novels—*The Spire* and *The Pyramid*. Third, he lost his beloved father (Carver, "William Golding," 390).

In November 1958, Alec Golding was diagnosed with cancer. Although the tumor was successfully removed, he died suddenly of a heart attack on December 12, 1958. According to Golding's daughter, he "was much affected by his father's death, and it added to his difficulties in writing. Later he recorded that he had shed more tears over his father than he had over any other human being. He had early on rejected his father's rationalist outlook, but was profoundly influenced by Alec's scientific curiosity and zest, and by his passionate commitment to social justice" (Carver, "William Golding," 390). His mother's death in August 1960 was not nearly as heavy a blow to Golding because she was "frail and with diminished faculties" (391).

Instead of working on a new novel in 1959, Golding settled for writing short works, publishing eight pieces in periodicals. That autumn, *Free Fall*, his fourth novel, appeared. The book tells the story of artist Sammy Mountjoy's search into his past to determine when he lost his innocence and chose to be evil. Of all Golding's novels, *Free Fall* "has been least praised—indeed, even panned—in the press . . . [although some critics] have praised it highly" (Biles, 78). Golding's friends and literary critics Ian Gregor and Mark Kinkead-Weekes claim that the book is "a considerable achievement" (170), but they also recognize that it is "the most elusive and difficult of Golding's novels so far" (138).

Although Golding's "personal struggles with writing" (Carver, "William Golding," 390) continued in 1960, he was able to produce a number of short works, including two autobiographical essays; the short story "Miss Pulkinhorn," a tale of a fanatic churchgoer whose charity masks her dark destructiveness; and many reviews.

Because of the popularity of *Lord of the Flies* with teachers and college professors, Golding became a campus cult figure in the 1960s. He served as the writer in residence at Hollins College, a women's liberal arts college in Virginia, during the 1961–1962 school year. He also wrote lectures that he delivered at prestigious colleges and universities such as Harvard, Vassar, Dartmouth, and the University of Pennsylvania; he worked on drafts of *The Spire*; and he published several items in periodicals. When he returned to England in 1962, he did not go back to Bishop Wordsworth's School. Instead, Golding made the daring decision to quit teaching in order to become a full-time writer, a job that provided no financial stability.

In spite of having the time to write, Golding did not produce much in 1963, publishing several essays in periodicals and still working on *The Spire*, a frustrating experience because he felt it was taking him too long to complete. Even though he struggled to write, Golding enjoyed many pleasures in 1963. One thing that "astonished and gratified" (Carver, "William Golding," 392) him was Peter Brook's film of *Lord of the Flies*, which was released in May. He also took delight in visiting with friends and acquaintances such as the English writer and translator, Peter Green. Like almost everyone who knew Golding, Green found him "to be an extraordinarily cheerful companion" (48). Seeing new lands always interested Golding, and he and Ann traveled to Greece and Russia.

The Spire was finally published in April 1964, five years after *Free Fall*. Inspired by the impressive cathedral in Salisbury, it is the story of Dean Jocelin, a medieval cleric who, believing God has chosen him to build a tower rising four hundred feet above Barchester Cathedral, pursues his goal with no concern for human lives. Golding was distressed when this work, which he considered "one of his very best novels" (Carver, "William Golding," 392), received mixed reviews. Many commentators found it "too complex and demanding to afford excitement" (Baker, 70).

In 1964, in order to help her husband succeed with his writing, Ann resigned from her part-time position as an arithmetic teacher at a boys' school, a job she thoroughly enjoyed. Since she was the person "he turned [to] for advice and criticism about his writing," his daughter says that "it was a great advantage to him to have her at home" (Carver, "William Golding," 392).

Even with her help, Golding wrote no new works in 1965 or 1966. However, he did collect a number of his essays and reviews into one volume, which was published as *The Hot Gates, and Other Occasional Pieces,* in 1965. It consists of essays about people and places, book reviews, accounts of his year in America, and two autobiographical essays—"Billy the Kid" and "The Ladder and the Tree." Another pleasing event for Golding was the performance of his play, *The Brass Butterfly,* in New York in December 1965. The following year, his country recognized his status by making him Commander of the Order of the British Empire (CBE), an honorary award given to individuals, such as actors, scientists, writers, artists, and politicians for personal bravery, achievement, or service to the United Kingdom.

Finally, after three years of hard work, Golding produced a new book, *The Pyramid*, in June 1967. This work of fiction, which analyzes the British class system, is also Golding's "first autobiographical work" (Tiger, 4). Although its title refers to Golding's fascination with Egypt, it is set in an English country town and told from the point of view of a middle-class boy, Oliver, who is "[t]otally conditioned by the pyramidical structure of society identical to that of Golding's childhood" (Friedman, 108). Golding recognized that this humorous work was not one of his best, regarding it as "a step backwards" (Gregor and Kinkead-Weekes, 221); but even so, he was disappointed by the harsh reviewers who suggested that Golding was losing his creative abilities. By 1980, however, views had somewhat changed, and several critics recognized that the "underestimated" novel (Tiger, 6) was "[m]uch more complex than most of its early reviewers and critics . . . found it to be" (Johnston, 92).

Golding now had enough money to buy a beautiful new sailing boat that he named *Tenace*. In July 1967 Golding took his wife, daughter, and three friends on a trip in his new, expensive boat. As they were sailing to France in crowded waters in the English Channel, the boat was run down, and it sank close to the Isle of Wight. Although the ship that hit them rescued everyone on board, Golding, "already depressed by personal difficulties, was shocked and badly shaken physically, as was his wife" (Carver, "William Golding," 393).

The Silent Years, 1968-1979

The next twelve years were very hard ones for Golding. He was depressed and angry with himself because he was unable to write a novel. Golding's depression "was exacerbated by family anxieties, particularly about his children"; and, without a new book, he also "worried about his finances" (Carver, "William Golding," 393). To make matters worse, he no longer sailed, an activity that had given him an outlet for his unhappiness. The wreck of the *Tenace* had marked the end of his life as a sailor; he never bought another boat. As a result of his frustrations, he began to drink heavily.

According to Golding's daughter, the years from 1968 to 1970 were "bleak in many ways, and the strain showed, partly in Golding's personal struggles with alcohol, partly

Golding experienced years of great professional success along with periods of personal depression.

in a degree of withdrawal from ordinary social life"; and once again he "began to find it more and more difficult to write, or to have faith in his writing" (Carver, "William Golding," 393). In 1970 he told an interviewer how upset he was that he could not write another novel: "I go on for a long time firmly in the belief that I'm never going to write another word. *Literally*, this is. You know, I can't think how anybody *can* write another word, and I reason with myself and say, 'Nonsense. Of course it will happen again.' And it doesn't, and I get very depressed" (Biles, 60).

In spite of his problems and his "grim moods at times," Carver says that Golding was "often busy and cheerful" and "took pleasure in travel, in music (particularly in playing the piano), and in friendship" (Carver, "William Golding," 393). One friend recalls spending many happy hours talking with Golding, whom he describes as "all humour [sic]. . . . His conversation flows with pun, sardonically humorous anecdote, and a quite unsardonically humorous presentation of himself." He also remembers Golding as a "clever performer" who played "electrifying" (Medcalf, "Bill," 34–35, 37) music on the piano.

Still struggling in both his professional and personal life in 1971, Golding began a journal to help get his imagination working once again. It reveals that, in spite of "his self-doubt and self-disgust, there was progress and satisfaction as well, and occasional happiness" (Carver, "William Golding," 394).

Although he was unable to write a novel, he published a new book, *The Scorpion God: Three Short Novels*, in October 1971. It contains a reprint of his 1956 story "Envoy Extraordinary" and two other short works, "Clonk Clonk" and "The Scorpion God." In "Clonk Clonk," set in prehistoric Africa, "the volatile, narcissistic, and fantasy-ridden virility of the male warriors is juxtaposed with the wisdom of women who . . . are matter-of-fact, cautious, devious in hiding their deceits, and outrageously skilled in their flattery of male vanity" (Tiger, 19). In "The Scorpion God," the ancient Egyptians, who arrogantly live by their preconceived ideas of the world, are entertained by the travel tales of the court jester, Liar, who tells them about strange things such as snow and people with pale skins. Liar, of course, triumphs in the end. Like *The Pyramid*, this book was not favorably received.

By now, Golding almost gave up trying to continue writing fiction and toyed with the idea of becoming a full-time journalist. However, his wife gave him the courage to keep on trying to fulfill his dreams, telling him "in the early 1970s that he would have to choose between literary journalism (tempting for many reasons) and being a novelist. She added that she personally believed he was a novelist. She demanded he take himself seriously, do justice to himself. And once more she provided him with courage" (Carver, "Harbour and Voyage," 54). As a result of her encouragement, Golding did not turn to journalism for full-time employment, although he did write some reviews in the 1970s. Instead, he began working on two novels, *Darkness Visible* and *Rites of Passage*.

Golding found some happiness during this decade. His family life was better because he worried less about his son, who, after his conversion to Roman Catholicism, was more content; he was cheered by the marriage of his daughter to Terrell Carver, an American graduate student at Oxford, in 1971; and he took pleasure in the birth of two grandsons, the first in 1976 and the second in 1979. He enjoyed traveling with his wife, taking trips to Australia, Italy, Yugoslavia, Switzerland, and Egypt. At home, he liked gardening and particularly enjoyed his water garden. He also vigorously practiced the piano. His daughter believed that his constant activities helped him become happier: "Older griefs—the loss of his father, the failure to be a great poet, the regrets about *Tenace*, and the feeling of futility and sadness in some aspects of his personal life—began to recede in the presence of successful activity" (Carver, "William Golding," 395).

Years of Renewed Creativity, 1979-1993

The year 1979 marked the beginning of a new period of creativity and a renewed critical interest in Golding's work. In 1979 and 1980, Golding was recognized as a creative genius "by two powerful novels appearing in such rapid succession that they seemed almost to have been written in tandem, but startlingly different, and producing very different responses" (Gregor and Kinkead-Weekes, 221–222). As the critics had suggested, the two books were actually written at the same time; Golding "worked on one for a few days and then reverted to the other" (Carver, "William Golding," 395).

Although *Darkness Visible*, published in October 1979, "remains perhaps the most challenging of all Golding's books," it is a work once more filled with the "intensity" (Gregor and Kinkead-Weekes, 255) of Golding's first works. The book's title comes from John Milton's description of the physical darkness of Hell in *Paradise Lost*. Lucifer, after being cast out of Heaven, surveys his new home in Hell and observes the terrible lightless place where, by means of "darkness visible," he sees nothing but "sights of woe" and "regions of sorrow," a place where "hope never comes" (Milton, 10; Book 1, ll. 63–66). Golding's novel begins in a type of Hell during the German blitzkrieg of London, when a fireman wonders whether the furnace he sees is the fire burning at the end of the world. Golding looks at the darkness found in the present-day world and in the characters influenced by the life of Matty, the hero, showing the human capacity for both good and evil. Critics have proclaimed the novel "the most powerful of all his metaphysical explorations, . . . an astonishingly original work, but difficult, contorted, obscure" (Gregor and Kinkead-Weekes, 272).

Unlike *Darkness Visible*, *Rites of Passage*, which came out in October 1980, is a humorous book that "dances along, much more light, bright, and sparkling, literary, linguistically inventive" (Gregor and Kinkead-Weekes, 272). The story, which critiques the British class system, is told by conceited Edmund Talbot, who travels on a ship to the Antipodes and becomes more mature when he is forced to see the role he played in causing a clergyman to shame himself and will himself to die. The English public loved this novel; in fact, "Not since *Lord of the Flies* had a Golding novel enjoyed such happy public recognition" (256). It "brought about a resurgence of interest in Golding's fiction" (Tiger, 27). Both books received prominent, national awards. *Darkness Visible* won the James Tait Black Memorial Prize, Scotland's most prestigious and the United Kingdom's oldest literary award for a novel. *Rites of Passage* earned the Booker McConnell Prize for the year's best novel, Britain's most prestigious literary award.

In his personal life, Golding was happier in the 1980s. His daughter writes that by September 1981 her father "had steadied himself" and "had begun to enjoy most of life again" (Carver, "William Golding," 395). Furthermore, because of the success of his two new novels, he no longer worried greatly about money. His family was important to him, and just as his parents had done before he and Ann became affluent, Golding and his wife generously took their children and grandchildren on month-long summer vacations to France or Spain almost every year from 1978 to 1992. Besides these summer vacations, Golding and Ann traveled extensively during the 1980s, going to Canada, the United States, Mexico, Malaysia, India, Japan, Singapore, Burma, Egypt, Austria, and Czechoslovakia. Back home in England, Golding

Rites of Passage was, unusually for Golding, who tended to look at the dark side, a humorous look at humanity.

took delight in the Wiltshire countryside and, when he was seventy years old, began horseback riding, a sport his daughter claims gave him "some of the experience of risk and independence which sailing had given him" (396).

He was also pleased that he published a new collection of reviews and essays, *A Moving Target*, in 1982. The title of the book comes from an essay of the same name in which Golding criticizes academics and critics for pigeonholing living writers into narrow categories instead of recognizing that their writings may change as the authors age. He sees himself as a moving target that constantly changes his artistic works and never writes the same thing twice.

In 1983, Golding was awarded the highest literary honor—the Nobel Prize in Literature. Unfortunately, his award was controversial, condemned by a number of people who did not think he deserved this recognition. For instance, Paul Gray, a critic for *Time* magazine, wrote that Golding "was decent but hardly in the Nobel Prize class" (Gray, 97). And the Swedish novelist Artur Lundkvist, a member of the Nobel committee, made the unprecedented declaration that the committee's decision was biased since Golding was "a little English phenomenon of no special interest" (quoted in Bufkin, 57). However, others commended the academy for selecting Golding. For example, writer Doris Lessing was "absolutely delighted" with the decision, and novelist John Fowles was convinced that Golding was "the best British novelist of his generation" (quoted in Keel and Webb, 1). Years later, Fowles still held his high opinion of Golding, declaring that he was personally "delighted" that this "affable, gentle man" who "shows a mixture of authority and reserve, with a distinct dry humour, a tiny hint of buried demon" was awarded the Nobel (Fowles, 149, 146, 147).

In spite of the controversy, Golding was elated to receive this recognition, but he refused to let himself become too egotistical. In his delightful, humorous, self-effacing conclusion to the "Nobel Lecture," he says that he must "remember not to take himself with unbecoming seriousness" but understand his "smallness in the scheme of things" ("Nobel Lecture 1983," 214). He then relates how two policemen, thinking he could not understand the printed words on a parking ticket, patiently helped him read the payment instructions. He was surprised when, after they had done so, they also congratulated him on winning the Nobel Prize for Literature.

The honor of winning this prize had negative side effects because Golding's private life was now filled with interviews, engagements, visitors, and sightseers. Before long, "Golding's admirers became a serious oppression, some of them stood at his garden gate in Wiltshire staring. . . . He fled down to Cornwall where he was born and where his mother came from. The house he bought, which was secluded [had a] drive [that] opened onto a road too busy for anyone to stand and stare" (Medcalf, "William Golding," 14).

Golding's reaction to the literary paparazzi is seen in his first novel after winning the Nobel Prize, *The Paper Men*, which appeared in 1984. This "mischievous fiction" (Tiger, 1) tells the story of an alcoholic novelist who is trying to evade a relentless critic-biographer who pursues him around the world. The "most socially realistic of all Golding's novels" (Everett, 111), *The Paper Men* is a different type of book than his earlier ones. Some commentators criticized it as "the least likely of all his works to attract new readers" because of three faults: "Its 'author'—drunken, womanizing, self-centred [*sic*], cynical, destructive and self-destructive—is the most rebarbative [*sic*] of all Golding's characters"; "the book's driving force appeared to be revenge on academic critics, particularly American ones"; and the language is "clichéd and quote-ridden, carelessly conversational, slangy, self-contemptuous" (Gregor and Kinkead-Weekes, 274).

However, writer Peter Green, having had experience with literary critics himself, feels differently, calling it "that hilariously funny squib" of "lethal accuracy" with "a mixture of high amusement and even higher exasperation" with the English critical professionals (54).

With his creative powers back, Golding published his third book of essays in 1985. This humorous book, *An Egyptian Journal*, is a record of his trip to Egypt in 1984; it contains new writings of descriptive comments as well as amusing details about the disasters of travel.

Once again Golding was recognized as a leading British writer, and he received two major honors. The literary world recognized his achievements in 1986 when Faber and Faber published *William Golding: The Man and his Books, A Tribute on his 75th Birthday*. Edited by John Carey, the book contains tributes from a number of critics and authors. In 1988 his country acknowledged his importance when he was knighted by Queen Elizabeth II. He became Sir William Gerald Golding.

Still energetic in his late seventies, Golding wrote two new novels before the end of the decade: *Close Quarters*, a sequel to *Rites of Passage*, was published in 1987; and *Fire Down Below*, a sequel to *Close Quarters*, appeared in 1989. Both works relate the further adventures of Edmund Talbot. Some critics do not think these two novels measure up to the original story because they are "soap-operatic" books that "seem to go on forever, piling episode relentlessly upon episode" (Boyd, 178). In 1991, the same year Golding celebrated his eightieth birthday, he was hard at work revising these three novels in order to join them into a single volume. *To the Ends of the Earth: A Sea Trilogy*, Golding's last book published during his lifetime, appeared in 1991. The next year he worked on "Scenes from a Life," an essay of events from his early years.

To the end of his life, Golding loved to travel. In the spring of 1990 when he was seventy-eight, he and his wife took a cruise on a luxurious ship around Southeast Asia. Two years later, in the summer of 1992, the entire Golding family—William, Ann, David, Judy, her husband, and their three children (the third born in 1983)—vacationed in Galicia, a seaside village in Spain. Shortly after they returned, Golding was diagnosed with malignant melanoma on his face, which was successfully removed just after Christmas.

By January 1993, Golding had recovered from his operation and was busy writing another novel. Peter Green, visiting him in June, found him "as energetic as ever" (Carver, "William Golding," 398). By June 18 "he had finished two drafts of the new novel, and intended to begin a further draft after the party [at their home that day]. However, on the morning of June 19, Golding's son-in-law, going to wake him, found he had died of heart failure" (398). His family was heartbroken. His daughter calls it "that terrible morning" and relates how his wife of over fifty years, on being told of his death, "stared at me, lost. Then she replied, 'But I've got so much to say to him'" (Carver, "Harbour and Voyage," 55). Before he was buried five days later in the churchyard at Bowerchalke, Ann had a stroke from which she never recovered. On January 1, 1995, eighteen months after Golding's death, Ann Golding died and was buried next to her husband in Bowerchalke.

Golding's last novel, *The Double Tongue*, was published in June 1995. This lighthearted book tells the story of a woman who is a prophetess at Delphi; it leaves readers wondering whether she is an authentic oracle or just a con artist talking nonsense in order to get money from gullible worshipers. In this final novel, Golding "is still trying new things. For the first time he writes from a woman's point of view. Also for the first time, his love of Greece, and of its literature, which he taught himself to read in the original, gets directly into his fiction" (Gregor and Kinkead-Weekes, 338). With this publication, the body of Golding's novels is complete.

Golding's many writings reveal his ideas about life and human beings, but they do not show the whole man. In some ways, the writer and the person are alike. Golding's friend Stephen Medcalf claims that "the man one talks to has all the interests and capacities of the writer of the novels. He is fascinated by technical contrivance; . . . by historical speculations; . . . by the evolution of mankind; by the sea; by the depths below our consciousness; by God." The man and the author are also similar in the "quickness of consciousness, and the changes of direction." But they are unlike in personality. Medcalf insists that "there is a great distinction between Bill and his daimon, his [inner spirit], his genius. . . . William Golding's daimon has little or no sense of humour; Bill is all humour" (Medcalf, "Bill," 34). For those who knew him, Golding was a very likable man of many interests, who had a quick mind, deep convictions, and an ever present sense of humor.

Germany was treated harshly in the Treaty of Versailles, the official end to World War I. Many believed that was an element in the Germans' seeking revenge on the Allied nations in World War II.

Chapter 2

Golding's Times

World War I, 1914-1918

William Golding was born three years before the beginning of World War I, the greatest event of the first two decades of the twentieth century. In the years before the war, tensions had been mounting between European nations because of political and economic competition. After the Germans invaded Belgium on their way to attack France, France's ally, Britain, declared war on the Central powers—Germany, Austria, Hungary, and Turkey—on August 4, 1914. The United States, which entered the war in 1917, and Russia also joined Britain and France. In 1917 the eastern front collapsed when the Bolshevik revolution began in Russia and the leader, Vladimir Lenin, urged the starving Russian soldiers to desert and return home. But the other Allies continued fighting another year and defeated the Central Powers, signing an armistice with Germany on November 11, 1918.

The Treaty of Versailles, which officially marked the end of the war, also set up the League of Nations, which was supposed to ensure peace in the world. In later life Golding reflected on the naivety of the supporters of this plan. He remarked that they thought it was "a Great Idea, in neon lighting. . . . Criminals and prisons and anything else you can talk about which deals with the seamy side of life were admitted to exist, but it was a dark thing down there; whereas the idea of the brotherhood of man, and all the rest of it, was somewhere up here, towards which everyone normally tended" (Biles, 35).

The First World War "changed fundamentally the ways in which people thought and wrote" (Peck and

Coyle, 224). Whereas before 1914, intellectuals, such as Golding's father, were "confident that human beings were rationally inclined and needed only a bit of clearsighted direction to construct the better world" (Day, 268), by 1918 they had lost their "traditional structure of values, understanding and reassurance" (Peck and Coyle, 228). During the war years, writers reflected the bleak feelings of despair felt by human beings, as seen in such works as James Joyce's *Dubliners* (1914) and T. S. Eliot's *Prufrock and Other Observations* (1917). Even though Golding was only a seven-year-old boy when the First World War ended, he adopted many of the beliefs about humanity that began to emerge at this time.

Inter-Bellum Years, 1918-1939

Although Great Britain was on the winning side, it paid heavily for the war, losing hundreds of thousands of young men and becoming economically devastated as "prices more than doubled, taxation reached about five times the prewar levels, and the burden of domestic and foreign debt increased 10 times between 1914 and 1918" (Day, 266). The situation became worse in the 1920s as laborers, angry over lack of jobs and poor wages, went on strike.

While the British were experiencing economic problems at home, political troubles arose with Ireland. After intense fighting in 1921, Southern Ireland, which was Roman Catholic, agreed to pledge allegiance to the British crown but be an independent nation called the Irish Free State. This did not suit the Protestant people of Northern Ireland, and that part of the country remained in the United Kingdom.

In 1929, the year before Golding entered Oxford University, the worldwide Great Depression began when the stock market crashed in the United States. Although about three million British workers were jobless by

In 1933, when Adolf Hitler first became chancellor of Germany, very few realized how powerful—and dangerous—he would become.

1932, the Golding family was not much affected by the Depression; Golding studied at Oxford in the 1930s, and his father maintained his teaching position.

Since European politicians were concentrating on their countries' economies, few leaders recognized the danger of the rise of Adolf Hitler and his Nazi Party in Germany. When he became chancellor in 1933, Hitler had a "very clear programme: to destroy the humiliation of Versailles and to reclaim the land removed from Germany" (Fraser, 691). Soon, he took away the civil liberties of Jews and enacted racist laws forbidding marriages between Jews and non-Jews. At the time, Golding says, he was "a very naïve person" who "didn't believe what [he] heard about Nazi Germany" (Biles, 30), but after fighting in World War II, he understood why Hitler was able to obtain power. Golding called Hitler "an evil genius" who "caught Germany just when everybody's sins were boiling over" (37) after the Treaty of Versailles. Explaining that the victors of World War I caused the Germans to feel inferior, Golding writes that "it is one of those terrifying things that at the moment when Germany was right for it, like the breaking of a boil, you get this man emerging. Then you get all the potentialities of man, all the beastly potentialities of man, given free rein, and there it was" (38).

During the mid–1930s, the British were caught up with affairs at home rather than politics abroad. In 1936 King George V died, leaving the throne to his oldest son, Edward, who wanted to marry an American divorcée, Mrs. Wallis Warfield Simpson. When the British government, the Church of England, and many British citizens objected, Edward VIII relinquished the throne to marry her, and his brother became George VI, who ruled until his death in 1952.

Meanwhile, the international problems did not go away. Besides Germany, Italy posed a problem, but neither the British nor the French wanted to alienate its leader, Benito Mussolini. To appease him, they gave him two-thirds of Ethiopia in late 1935. This action empowered Hitler, who declared in 1936 that he would no longer follow the Versailles agreement. By the time Neville Chamberlain became prime minister of England in 1937, Hitler's aggression was becoming more apparent, but Chamberlain thought he could deal with the German leader and avoid war. Therefore, in 1938, after Hitler seized Austria and demanded part of Czechoslovakia, Chamberlain and the French premier sacrificed Czechoslovakia when Hitler agreed to claim no additional land. Returning home, Chamberlain waved the peace pact and naively declared, "Peace in our time" (Day, 266).

During these decades, artists reflected the times. In the 1920s writers such as D. H. Lawrence, E. M. Forster, Ezra Pound, James Joyce, W. B. Yeats, Virginia Woolf, and T. S. Eliot articulated the pessimistic mood that had begun with World War I. Eliot's *The Waste Land* (1922) and Woolf's *Mrs. Dalloway* (1925) express the cynical view that people live meaningless but desperate lives. In the next decade of failing economies and rising dictatorial leaders, writers, including W. H. Auden, Noël Coward, George Orwell, J. R. R. Tolkien, and Aldous Huxley, were concerned with contemporary political and social issues. For example, Huxley's *Brave New World*, the most popular novel in England of the 1930s, described the negative role science might play in establishing dictatorships and controlling human lives. With the world in turmoil, a number of intellectuals searched for some sort of order to and meaning in life. Some, such as T. S. Eliot and C. S. Lewis, turned traditional, going back to Western culture and Christianity. Others, such as the American John Steinbeck, who wrote *The Grapes of Wrath*, turned to communism as a way to solve social ills. Although Golding did not advocate communism, at this time he did believe that "if we should establish a perfect social system, we would then, in effect, have perfect people" (Biles, 30), a view he rejected after World War II.

While writers were examining social issues, musicians were discarding old styles of music. Young people began listening to jazz, a new style that had started with black musicians in New Orleans in the 1920s and quickly spread throughout the United States and then to England. It is quite probable that the musical Golding family listened to jazz on the wireless set (radio) Alec Golding put in his home in the 1920s.

World War II, 1939-1945

In 1939, Germany seized the rest of Czechoslovakia and invaded Poland. Chamberlain still tried to appease Hitler, but when Hitler remained defiant, Britain and France declared war on Germany on September 3. Chamberlain was voted out of office in May 1940 and Winston Churchill, who early on had seen the dangers of Nazi Germany, became Britain's new prime minister.

Churchill was committed to defeating Hitler. By June France fell to the German military, and the British stood alone against Hitler's powerful forces, which now turned their attention to conquering the island nation. The Luftwaffe began the aerial bombing of London, where "[t]housands of civilians perished, and much of central London was destroyed" (Day, 266). But the British refused to be beaten; encouraged by Churchill's appeal to make this their "finest hour" (Peck and Coyle, 267), they prepared to invade the continent. Twenty-nine-year-old Golding, a husband and father, joined the Royal British Navy in 1940 to help the British cause.

The war became a worldwide conflict in 1941 after Germany invaded Russia and Japan attacked Pearl Harbor in Hawaii. The Allies squeezed Germany, with Russia attacking from the east and Britain, Canada, and the United States coming from the west. On June 6, 1944, the combined Western Allies staged a daring, bloody invasion of Normandy in France; Golding fought on this day, known as D-day, which marked the beginning of the end for Germany. On May 8, 1945, the war ended in Europe. Several months later, after atomic bombs destroyed Hiroshima and Nagasaki, Japan also surrendered and World War II was over.

Britain took a heavy toll for its victory. It lost many people, with "over 400,000 killed or missing, and about the same number of wounded" (Day, 267). It also lost much wealth. The war cost more than sixteen billion pounds "and the national debt more than trebled" (267). And Britain lost prestige. Now a debtor nation, it no longer retained its position of power, replaced by the United States and the Soviet Union, which emerged as the most powerful nations of the world.

Before the war ended, Britain helped create the United Nations, the new worldwide peace-keeping force. By this

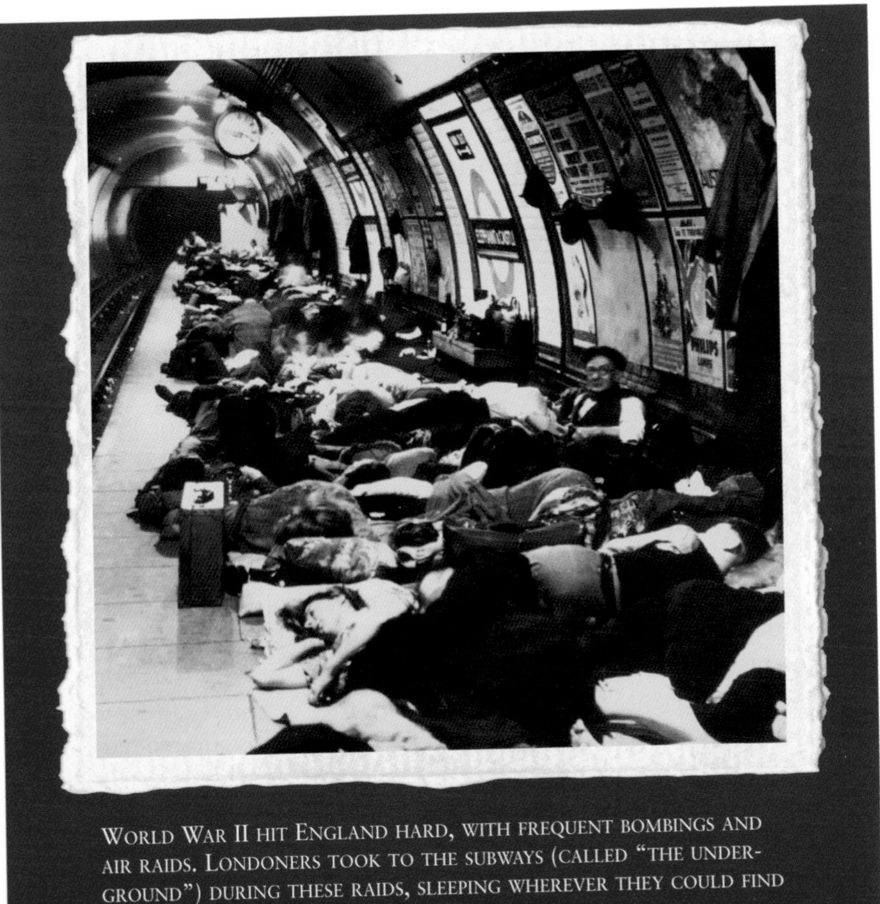

WORLD WAR II HIT ENGLAND HARD, WITH FREQUENT BOMBINGS AND AIR RAIDS. LONDONERS TOOK TO THE SUBWAYS (CALLED "THE UNDERGROUND") DURING THESE RAIDS, SLEEPING WHEREVER THEY COULD FIND SPACE ON THE STATION PLATFORMS.

time, Golding, realizing "how horrific people could be" (Biles, 34), was convinced that an organization based on human beings' social perfectibility was doomed to failure. He had witnessed firsthand the atrocities of human beings—he had been at the sinking of the *Bismarck*, and he had seen thousands of young men mowed down during the D-day landings and the invasion of Walcheren.

Post War Years, 1945-1993

World Events

The United States and the Soviet Union became bitter enemies following World War II as the Soviets helped communists seize control of most of the countries in Eastern Europe. America, aided by Great Britain, became the defender of non-Communist nations. This struggle between democracy and communism became known as the cold war. Fighting broke out in 1950 when Communist North Korea, backed by the Soviet Union, invaded South Korea; and America and Great Britain fought to stop the spread of communism. When the Vietnam War was fought in the 1960s and 1970s, the British did not join American forces.

As the cold war escalated, the two superpowers began a missile-development race, which concerned Golding. In 1963, when he visited Moscow with other English, French, and Russian writers, "politics greatly affected the literary discussions" (Carver, "William Golding," 392) since America and the Soviet Union had signed a test-ban treaty. In spite of the pact, the arms race continued. When Ronald Reagan was elected president of the United States in 1980, he extended the race into space, announcing that he was going to create a defensive nuclear shield over the American continent. However, by the end of the decade, President Reagan, with the aid of Britain's Prime Minister Margaret Thatcher, helped bring about the end of Russian Communism, and the iron curtain that had divided

Europe for decades was gone. In 1990 the new president of Russia, Boris Yeltsin, announced that there was no "Soviet Union," only a "Commonwealth of Independent States" (Fraser, 768).

Life in Great Britain

As a result of World War II, the exhausted British nation faced two primary outcomes—the creation of the welfare state and the loss of its empire. In 1945, when the Labour Party, which was the party Golding's father and wife adamantly supported, came into power, it turned Britain into a welfare state. Since the country faced huge war debts and its economy was ruined by the war, the government felt it needed to help its citizens; therefore, it

The ascension of Margaret Thatcher as prime minister marked a time of economic recovery for Britain and for Golding, though that would seem to have been coincidental. In this photo, Thatcher makes a speech at the White House as President Ronald Reagan stands by.

expanded the social security system, providing "cradle-to-grave" (Day, 267) health, education, and welfare for every worker. To help pay for these services and to stimulate the economy, the new government began to socialize industries. It closed down private businesses—banks, coal mines, the iron and steel industry, the railroads, and the trucking industry—and placed them under the government's control. But the party's efforts failed to bring back Britain's economy, which continued to decline in the following decades. Golding, who was able to return to his teaching job after the war, did not seem to be adversely affected by the bad economy. One unexpected outcome that must have pleased Golding was the partial breakdown of Britain's rigid class system, because the well-to-do had reduced incomes due to the poor economy while workers had a better standard of living. As a youth, Golding was well aware that people's positions in life depended on their class, for he had felt the pangs of his inferior position as the son of a middle-class man. As an adult, he criticized the class system in *The Pyramid* and *Rites of Passage*.

The second big effect of the war was the loss of the vast British empire. Bankrupt England could no longer afford to run its huge colonial empire; therefore, when colonies insisted on independence, the British agreed to their demands. Between 1947 and 1963, Great Britain gave independence to "over 600,000,000 people in countries all over the globe" (Day, 267). With this loss of the empire, British prestige declined.

While the British Commonwealth was fragmenting, Britain also lost the Suez Canal, which was seized by Egypt in 1955. Although the canal owners, Britain and France, attacked Egypt, they did not succeed in retaking it.

Britain began to recover economically with Winston Churchill's return to office as prime minister in 1951. When he retired in 1955, more people had good jobs and industry was flourishing. The people were also cheered by the reign of a new monarch, Queen Elizabeth II, who ascended to the throne in 1953. But the good times did not last for long. With the Labour Party in power throughout most of the 1960s and 1970s, Britain faced monetary problems. Taxes were raised, wages were capped, and the pound was devalued. As a result, laborers engaged in strike after strike. Adding to problems at home were the tensions between Protestants and Roman Catholics in Northern Ireland, which became acute in the late 1960s and 1970s. During these decades, Golding was quite depressed and, as a result, did not actively engage in political affairs.

By 1979 "British industrial productivity had reached dramatic new lows. Britain was known as the Sick Man of Europe and was being held to ransom by the unions" (Fraser, 757) because the unions did not allow companies to keep pace with technology. But that year, which, ironically, was the same year Golding made a comeback by finally publishing a novel, Britain started to recover when Margaret Thatcher became prime minister. Almost immediately, she tried to revitalize the economy by returning industries to private citizens. As trade unions lost power, Great Britain started to do better economically. She also tried to do away with the welfare state, demanding that people put in some effort on their own behalf instead of looking to the government for assistance.

Although the 1960s and 1970s were turbulent, they were also a progressive period, the "heyday of ideas and idealism" (Fraser, 744). Scientific discoveries increased. New technology created the *Concorde* airplane, which was able to fly faster than the speed of sound. Space exploration became a reality: satellites were placed in space in the late 1950s; in 1961 Russian Yuri Gagarin and American Alan B. Shepard Jr. became the first two people to travel in space; and on July 20, 1969, American Neil Armstrong became the first person to walk on the moon. Science also increased medical knowledge; the first heart transplant operation occurred in 1967, and the first test-tube baby was born in 1978. Because of the developments in the physical and natural sciences, many people became idealistic, believing that through science the world and people could get better and better, a view Golding discredited. As he shows through his character Piggy in *Lord of the Flies*, Golding was highly distrustful of the optimistic view that science could solve all problems, calling Piggy "naïve, short-sighted, and rationalist, like most scientists" and explaining that "Piggy understands society less than almost anyone there at all. He's a scientist" (Biles, 12–13).

During these decades, idealistic students made universities the "hotbeds of radical thought" (Fraser, 744). There was great permissiveness both on and off campus—women wore short skirts; homosexuality was legalized; no-fault divorce was granted; and the nation's youth advocated for revolution in response to the Vietnam War (745–752).

In spite of the new radicalism, British citizens rallied around the government leaders in the early 1980s. In July 1981 they were thrilled to watch Prince Charles wed Lady Diana Spencer. A majority also approved of Prime Minister Margaret Thatcher's decision to fight Argentina for control of the Falklands after Argentina invaded these British-ruled islands. However, less than a decade later, Thatcher was voted out of office. The new leadership was not as strong, and by September 1992 Britain's economy was "in tatters" (Fraser, 773). When Golding died in 1993, the British people were engaged in a new wave of disillusionment because of "long hospital waiting lists," "decaying schools," "poor social services," and bad roads filled with "potholes" (773).

Literature and the Arts

Like many people in these decades after the war, musicians were taking a stand against the status quo. Rock 'n' roll, then a new form of music, became popular with teenagers in the mid-1950s, with Elvis Presley the leading artist. The new rock group that came from Liverpool, England, the Beatles, the most popular singers in rock music history, probably had the greatest impact on the arts in the 1960s. Since then, the United Kingdom has produced other popular types of music, particularly rock music with well-known artists such as the Rolling Stones and Led Zeppelin, and heavy metal bands such as Iron Maiden.

Like musicians, literary artists of the last half of the twentieth century also rebelled against established society, writing about lonely, disillusioned people who suffered because of a corrupt society. In America, J. D. Salinger's popular *The Catcher in the Rye* told of an adolescent fighting against a world of phony adults, and Sylvia Plath's *The Bell Jar* related the story of a vulnerable girl trapped because of society's expectations of conformity. English writers were also antiestablishment. For example, dramatist Tom Stoppard, in *Rosencrantz and Guildenstern Are Dead*, focused "on little men in a world beyond their comprehension" (Peck and Coyle, 275); poet Ted Hughes, who became poet laureate of England, showed "the pretensions of civilization" (283). Unlike most of his contemporaries, William Golding did not view people as victims of a corrupt society. In fact, he said, "I was writing *Lord of the Flies* because of my feeling that people had been looking at systems rather than at people" (Biles, 50). Instead of focusing on the sins of society, Golding looked at the wickedness found within every individual, revealing a world destroyed because of fallen humans.

In spite of all the changes and advancements that occurred during his nearly eighty-two years of life, Golding did not think that human beings were capable of change. Although he recognized that people could change their environments and their societies, he believed they could not alter their inherent, evil natures.

One only has to say "Lord of the Flies" for people to instantly get the reference to an anarchic world in which rules of decency no longer apply. This 1990 movie version made the drama real for a new generation.

Chapter 3

Lord of the Flies

Lord of the Flies, PUBLISHED IN 1954, is William Golding's best known and most popular novel. Critic Patrick Reilly claims that "*Lord of the Flies* is one of the most important texts of the twentieth century, for both literary and extraliterary reasons. It is a fable vital to our times for three reasons: the urgency of its questions, the audacity of its answers, and the formal originality of its investigation" (7). Reilly points out that Piggy's questions about the nature of human beings, "What are we? Humans? Or animals? Or savages?" (*Lord of the Flies*, 79), are important in this dangerous century of genocide, terrorists, suicide bombers, and schoolroom murderers. He further argues that Ralph's pleas for insight, "[W]hat's wrong? . . . [W]hat makes things break up like they do?" (124), are significant questions because the responses given can affect the entire world. Golding's answers to these questions are not easy, pat formulas about human progress or perfection that can come about with scientific advancement, good governments, or strong economies. Instead of looking at society for solutions to human ills, Golding examines basic human nature and helps his readers gain "a renewed sense of the difficulty and complexity of the moral life and the opacity, perhaps even the evil, of people" (Reilly, 10). Through *Lord of the Flies*, Golding forces readers to recognize the truth of the human soul so that they can realistically understand themselves, other people, and the world.

Plot

During a nuclear war, a plane carrying a group of evacuated British schoolboys has been shot down, and the boys land on a tropical island, where Ralph meets Piggy. When Ralph finds a conch shell, Piggy suggests that he blow it to call the other survivors together. One of the boys that appears is Jack Merridew, the leader of a cathedral school choir that arrives at the assembly marching in military style. The boys roughly divide into two groups—the "littluns," boys about six years of age, and the "biguns," boys aged about ten to twelve. They elect Ralph to be their leader, even though Jack thinks he is the better choice. After Ralph decides that they need to know the nature of the island, he, Jack, and Simon take an investigative trip.

At the second meeting, the explorers relate that the island is an uninhabited, good place, well supplied with fruit, pigs (which Jack decides to hunt and kill for food), and fresh water. The optimistic boys decide to make and follow rules until they are rescued. However, the happy meeting is marred when one small boy confesses that he is afraid of a "beastie," a snakelike creature he says lives in the jungle. Although Ralph insists that there isn't a beast, the boys remain unconvinced. However, they focus on getting rescued when Ralph says that they need to start a signal fire on the mountain to alert a passing ship. Immediately, the boys race to the mountain, collect a huge pile of wood, and use the lenses of Piggy's glasses to get a flame. But the fire rages out of control, destroying a large section of the island and killing one of the littluns. The boys decide to build a smaller fire from then on, and Jack and his choir members volunteer to keep it going.

While Ralph and Simon spend their time building huts for shelters, Jack searches for pigs. He enlists the help of his choir, including those assigned to keep the signal fire going. While they are hunting, the fire goes out. Back at the beach, Ralph spies a ship, but since the fire is dead, the ship does not stop. When the hunters return victorious with their first pig kill, Ralph confronts Jack about neglecting the fire.

Ralph calls another assembly to try to get the boys to follow the rules so they can be rescued. During this meeting, some of the littluns tell of their fear of a beast that comes from the water. Although Ralph once again insists that there is no beast, Jack promises that he and his hunters will look for it. When Simon suggests that the beast may be the boys themselves, he is scorned.

That night, unknown to the boys, a parachutist is killed in an aerial battle and his body lands on the mountain. Trapped by his gear, his body moves up and down with the breeze. When Sam and Eric see his dead body, they mistake it for the beast and run to tell the boys. Ralph and the other biguns hunt for the beast; when they see the dead parachutist, they too think it is the beast. Now all the boys live in fear. Jack, thinking he should be chief since he is a hunter and can protect the others, leaves Ralph's group to form his own society. More and more boys leave Ralph to join Jack and his hunters, who paint their faces, hunt, and perform ritualistic dances. When they kill a sow, they offer the beast a peace offering by placing the pig's head on a stick that is sharpened at both ends. To roast the meat, they invade Ralph's group to steal fire, and they invite all the boys to a feast.

Only mystic Simon refuses to accept the existence of a physical beast. Alone in the woods next to the bloody pig's head, Simon listens to the head on the stake. It becomes the Lord of the Flies, saying, "Fancy thinking the Beast was something you could hunt and kill! . . . You knew, didn't you? I'm part of you?" (128). Simon then loses consciousness. After he recovers he forces himself up the mountain to discover the nature of the "beast" and finds the dead parachutist, whom he releases. He then attempts to join the others to tell them about his discovery.

Meanwhile, all the boys, including Ralph and Piggy, are in Jack's camp enjoying the pig feast and participating in the pig-killing dance. When Simon stumbles into the camp during the dance, the boys beat him to death, thinking he is the beast.

The next night Jack and two hunters attack Ralph's camp and steal Piggy's glasses, leaving Ralph unable to keep a signal fire going because he no longer has Piggy's glasses with which to start a fire. Ralph, Piggy (carrying the conch), and the twins Sam and Eric, who are the only

IN THIS 1963 FILM VERSION OF *LORD OF THE FLIES* DIRECTED BY PETER BROOK THE BOYS DRESS UP AS THE SAVAGES THEY HAVE QUICKLY BECOME.

remaining members of Ralph's group, go to Jack to demand that he give back Piggy's glasses. As Piggy pleads for Jack to do the right thing, Roger releases a huge boulder that strikes Piggy, killing him and shattering the conch. The hunters capture Sam and Eric, leaving Ralph totally alone, and Jack now declares himself chief.

The next day Jack's tribe covers the island to find and kill Ralph. To smoke him out of his hiding place, they start a fire that quickly spreads throughout the island. At the last moment, as Ralph runs on the beach pursued by Jack and his savages, he falls at the feet of a British naval officer, who, seeing the smoke, has arrived to rescue the boys. The officer is disappointed that the boys haven't managed better, while Ralph weeps for the loss of innocence as he recognizes the darkness of man's heart.

Themes and Issues

The Inner Evil of All Human Beings

In *Lord of the Flies* Golding argues against the commonly held belief that human beings are moral creatures who can be perfected as long as they are not corrupted and victimized by an immoral society. Instead, he shows that all humans have good and evil within themselves. He describes the novel as "an attempt to trace the defect of society back to the defects of human nature" (quoted in Epstein, 204).

People's natural inclination toward evil is seen most obviously in Jack and his tribe of hunters. Although their stated reason for killing pigs—to provide meat for everyone—seems altruistic, the boys are also hunting because they enjoy killing and torturing living creatures. In the first pig kill, their delight in overpowering and killing a living animal is apparent as they excitedly describe the event. Their joy becomes ritualized in their chant: "*Kill the beast! Cut her throat! Spill her blood!*" (58). After killing a pig once, the hunters want to do more than merely kill; they wish to inflict pain. This desire is seen first when Robert pretends to be the pig and the boys start jabbing at him with a spear and brandishing a knife. In the second pig killing, the boys brutally kill the sow, torturing it in a rapelike fashion before cutting its throat. After this they accidentally murder Simon, whom they think is a beast, as they let their savage emotions take control of their reason. Killing Piggy is even easier for Roger, who purposely releases the rock to squash him. By this time the boys are so hardened that when Jack screams at Ralph, "That's what you'll get!" (163) and hurls a spear at him, no one objects. By the end of the novel, the boys have become so diabolical that they hunt Ralph like they hunted the pigs.

Although Golding demonstrates humans' capacity for evil most completely in Jack and the hunters, he also shows that evil is not confined to one group of people, because even the two good boys, Ralph and Piggy, participate in Simon's murder.

Adults are even worse than the boys are since they commit evil on a larger scale by waging a war in which atom bombs are exploded. The war is the reason the boys are marooned on the island in the beginning of the novel. Because of the war, an adult intrudes on the island in the middle of the novel when an air fight occurs over the island and a dead parachutist lands on the mountain. At the end of the book, an officer engaged in war rescues the boys, but he brings them back to a world in which there is great destruction.

Although Golding shows that everyone—from the youngest child to the adults—has innate evil, he also makes it clear through Simon, Ralph, and Piggy that human beings do not have to be controlled by it. Simon recognizes his capacity for evil but constantly does good deeds, and less saintly Ralph and Piggy control their inner evil tendencies with reason and morality.

Thus, Golding shows that some people, such as Jack, become more and more depraved when there are no consequences for their actions, while others, like Ralph, recognize the tendency toward evil in themselves and seek to contain it. At the end of the novel Ralph grieves over the evil he has discovered in the human heart, an evil he had never suspected before his time on the island. Realizing that evil is an active element in people, Ralph weeps at the end of the novel, portraying Golding's theme of *Lord of the Flies*, which is "grief, sheer grief, grief, grief" ("Moving Target,"163). This "grief which Golding expresses and powerfully elicits in the novel is grief at man's very nature and the nature of the world, grief that the boys, and we too, are 'suffering from the terrible disease of being human'" (Boyd, 3).

Loss of Innocence

When people live in a safe, civilized society, they often can remain ignorant about the true nature of human beings. This leads to disaster because humans who are naive more easily give in to evil. Golding's boys begin in a state of innocence, seeing people as well-intentioned and good-hearted. They act like well-behaved children who desire to work together in order to be rescued, and they innocently occupy their time by swimming in the lagoon. But soon they become vicious hunters, roaming the jungle searching for pigs to torture and kill. They are so enamored with hunting that they no longer wish to keep a signal fire going so they can return to their homes.

Golding shows that people need to understand their evil tendencies because this knowledge leads to maturity. By the end of the novel, Ralph has gone through this painful process of maturation, and he "wept for the end of innocence, the darkness of man's heart, and the fall through the air of the true wise friend called Piggy" (182).

The Role of Fear in People's Lives

By making the children terrified of an imaginary beast, Golding looks at how fear of the unknown causes people to act irrationally and even give up their morals. When the little boys first imagine that the jungle vines are really snakelike "beasties," Ralph immediately rejects this notion. However, Jack leaves open the possibility that such a beast may exist, saying, "Ralph's right of course. There isn't a snake-thing. But if there was a snake we'd hunt it and kill it. We're going to hunt pigs and get meat for everybody. And we'll look for the snake too" (28). When Ralph continues to insist that "there isn't a beast" (29), the boys are able to work together to create a peaceful society. But the fear persists. Even Jack becomes afraid, telling the assembly, "'If you're hunting sometimes you catch yourself feeling as if—' He flushed suddenly. 'There's nothing in it of course. Just a feeling. But you can feel as if you're not hunting, but being hunted, as if something's behind you all the time in the jungle'" (43).

As the fear of a beast becomes more pronounced the longer the boys live on the island, civilization breaks down. When the littluns tell of their fear of a beast that comes out of the sea, Golding shows that human capacity for evil cannot be controlled or eliminated by humane governments as Ralph, trying to be democratic, "Ludicrously, ineptly, damagingly . . . determines that a vote on its existence should be taken" (Tiger, 39). Ralph does recognize that fear of the unknown beast has caused the democratic society to crumble: "Things are breaking up. I don't understand why. We began well; we were happy. . . . Then people started getting frightened" (70). His analysis is accurate; the meeting ends as the boys refuse to follow the rules, and Jack stomps away in defiance of Ralph and Piggy.

In the next chapter, "Beast from the Air," the boys' society totally erodes. When the boys, Sam and Eric, known as Samneric, run down the mountain to report that they have seen the beast, even Ralph becomes afraid. Although the boys at first band together to hunt the beast, their fear soon causes them to abandon the reasonable society offered by Ralph and to flee to the tyrannical society of Jack, who offers them protection. Even though Jack tries to appease the beast by offering it a pig's head on a stake, the boys still live in terror. This fear causes their dark natures to surface, as they savagely kill Simon, whom they irrationally think is the beast; Roger murders Piggy; and they attempt to kill Ralph.

The fear of an unknown beast, then, causes the boys to willingly give up their freedom and idyllic life to be dominated and threatened by a dictator who promises protection from the unknown. In the process, they abandon their morals and their reason.

The Failure of Science

Although modern men and women regard science and technology highly, Golding shows the dangers of "a naïve and potentially disastrous faith in science" through Piggy (Reilly, 8), dismissing this well-meaning, decent boy as the kind of person who will end up in a white coat at Los Alamos, a town in New Mexico that is a center for nuclear research (Biles, 14). Rational Piggy is the perfect scientific boy, who believes that people "know what goes on and if there's something wrong, there's someone to put it right" (72). But Golding shows that his view of life is wrong, because Piggy's rational approach to life does not convince the boys to act as he thinks they should, and he is unable to lead them. Furthermore, Piggy fails to understand people and their motives. For example, when Jack and his hunters raid the beach, Piggy thinks they have come for the conch instead of his glasses. And when he reasonably goes to get them back, he is killed. Thus, Golding shows that Piggy is a "weaker sort of intellectual" (Oldsey and Weintraub, 26) whose "chief handicap is his unfounded trust in a rational universe administered by rational man" (Reilly 114). As Boyd argues, his "rationalism is as inadequate as his grammar. His reason cannot control the boys, his belief that science can explain everything makes him unable to comprehend the reality of the Beast, his democracy crumbles before the onslaught of . . . Jack, intuitively adept at using the Beast for his own ends. Piggy may be the brains of the outfit but the Beast in Roger, by smashing his skull, makes those brains useless" (Boyd, 8–9). Therefore, in *Lord of the Flies*, Golding "heretically insists that science is *not* the paramount human activity, defiantly ranking philosophy, history, and aesthetic perception as both higher and more essential pursuits" (Reilly, 8). In fact, Golding even suggests that Piggy's view of life "is one of the most dangerous errors" (Boyd, 9).

The Indifference of Nature

Critic S. J. Boyd claims that "Golding is determined to disabuse us not only of naïve optimism about the nature of children but also of the sort of faith in the goodness of all things natural" (Boyd, 6). He does this by placing the boys on an Eden-like island, a lush place with ripe fruit hanging within reach, fresh water flowing from the mountain, and a warm climate. Here they are free to do as they please with no grown-ups to tell them what to do. But this tropical island is not a perfect place. For one thing, it is a place of fear, as the boys imagine a "snake-thing" (27) inhabiting it. Also, without proper lavatory facilities or a balanced diet, the littluns become "filthily dirty" and suffer from "a sort of chronic diarrhoea [*sic*]" (49). The boys themselves contribute to the filth on the island, a situation that concerns Ralph as he complains about the boys' failure to use one area as a place to relieve themselves: "Now people seem to use anywhere. Even near the shelters and the platform" (69). As the children get dirtier, the littluns cry about their miserable circumstances, and the big boys become more violent and cruel. "The boys' return to nature, then, is not an idyll but a nightmare" (Boyd, 9).

Analysis

Setting

The novel takes place on a boat-shaped island in a tropical climate. Near the lagoon is a beach where the meetings take place. Farther inland is a mountain where the boys first set their signal fire. Much of the island is a jungle with thick vines the boys call "creepers." The pigs live here, and Simon has his secluded place here as well. There is also a fruit orchard on the island where the boys gather food. At one end of the main island is another island, a rock that is almost detached, which the boys name "castle rock." It becomes Jack's camping ground, and it is the site of Piggy's death.

Structure

Golding calls this novel a fable, a fictional story that teaches a moral lesson. Although most fables, such as Aesop's, use talking animals, Golding fills his fable with human children. And instead of ending with a simple proverb that clearly states a moral about how to live, Golding's message is a much more complex one—that evil lives in every human being.

Critic Virginia Tiger maintains that the novel "consists of two movements told from two points of view: in the first the events are seen from the point of view of the childish protagonist. . . . In the second movement, the coda which concludes the text, the reader encounters events from a new point of view, that of an adult officer, who is completely unaware and largely indifferent to the suffering" (Tiger, 36). The coda, therefore, is "a deliberate device by which to throw the story into focus" (Peter, 26). By providing a new point of view, the coda accomplishes three purposes: first, "it reminds us that the characters we have been seeing as hunters and killers are only children, while the officer's patronizing air alerts us to the fact that precisely the same horrors are being re-enacted in the adult world"; second, through Ralph's tears, readers realize his "bitter understanding of the evil that resides within humanity"; and third, Ralph's understanding of human beings' evil "provides a darkly ironic counterpoint to the officer's helpful comment: 'I know. Jolly good show. Like The Coral Island'" (McCarron, 7). Until the coda, the boys, and also most readers, wrongly believe that grown-ups can help the boys. But the coda, told from the point of view of a naive adult who rescues the boys and returns them to the grown-up world of nuclear war and destruction, painfully reveals that "the child's world on the island is a painful microcosm of the adult world, and the ruin they bring upon themselves is widespread" (Tiger, 37).

Characters

Ralph

Handsome and good-natured, Ralph, whose name means "good omen" in Anglo-Saxon (Loughead, 138), is the leader of the boys. The son of a naval officer, this middle-class boy is the elected chief of the group, chosen because of his attractiveness and his size (he is built like a boxer), as well as the fact that he has the conch, which the boys regard as a symbol of authority. Ralph is basically a good boy. He attempts to establish a fair, democratic, peaceful government on the island. He also takes responsibility for the welfare of others by building huts, trying to keep the fire going, and making rules to keep their food and water clean even when he would sooner be hunting with Jack or swimming in the lagoon.

However, Ralph is not a perfect boy. Sometimes he would rather fit in with the crowd than do the right thing. For example, at the beginning of the story, he tells the other boys that the fat boy is called Piggy, even though he has promised not to tell. Later, he gets caught up in the mob mentality as he participates in Simon's murder. However, he redeems himself somewhat by acknowledging his guilt.

Although he is not as intellectual as Piggy, not as intuitive as Simon, and not as aggressive as Jack, he gains the respect of readers because "he has courage, he has good intelligence, he is a diplomat (in assuaging Piggy's feelings and dividing authority with Jack), and he elicits perhaps our greatest sympathy (when hounded across the island)" (Oldsey and Weintraub, 21).

Jack

Jack Merridew is the most evil person on the island. Physically, he "is distinguished by his ugliness and his red hair, a traditional demonic attribute" (Rosenfield, 121). In Hebrew, the name Jack means "supplanter" (Loughead, 99), a person who forcefully takes over another's position, as Jack does in the novel. From the beginning Jack is seen as a ruthless dictator. The head choir boy at a cathedral school, Merridew, as he first calls himself, forces his choir to march along the hot, tropical beach in tight military formation while dressed in heavy black chorister robes with square black caps trimmed with silver crosses.

An arrogant boy, Jack feels that his position as an upper-middle-class choir leader from a Cathedral school entitles him to lead the island group and to scorn those he feels are not his equals, especially Piggy, whom he constantly threatens and intimidates. He feels a sense of superiority, declaring, "We're English; and the English are best at everything" (34). Critic J. S. Boyd remarks that Jack's "self-congratulatory attitude [about being English] is dangerous because it allows the Devil to go to work, evils to be perpetuated, under cover of the belief that English people are good, decent and fair-minded" (Boyd, 12).

Jack's greatest desire is to hunt and kill. When he becomes a hunter, he physically changes, turning almost bestial. He seems like an animal with "his nose only a few inches from the humid earth" as he "dog-like" crawls along "on all fours," no longer wearing his cloak and clothes but only a "pair of tattered shorts held up by his knife-belt" (39). Like an animal he smells "with flared nostrils," while his eyes are "bolting and nearly mad" (39). Soon, he covers up his human qualities, hiding behind a painted mask, becoming "finally freed from all the repressions of his past" (Rosenfield, 126).

Jack gains power "when the children's fears distort the natural objects around them" (Rosenfield, 126). He sets up a dictatorship, a form of government his followers willingly accept in order to receive his protection. Jack is an ideal dictator, possessing "that charismatic attraction so frequently found in the 20th-century dictator. Combined with this are his lust for power, worship of physical prowess and contempt for the ineffectual speech-making of Ralph's parliamentarian assembly" (Kearns, 151). Furthermore, Jack knows how to manipulate people, perceiving "almost intuitively the use of mask, dance, ritual, and propitiation to ward off—and yet encourage simultaneously—fear of the unknown: Propitiation is a recognition not only of the need to pacify but also of something to be pacified" (Oldsey and Weintraub, 23).

Although Jack is a power-mad dictator, Golding is clear that Jack is not an unusual person; he shows that all people have the capability of becoming as evil as Jack is. His name shows that he is an everyman type of figure since *Jack* is a "familiar by-form of the name *John*; hence, a generic proper name for any representative of the common people" ("Jack," 162).

Piggy

Smart, logical Piggy is an outsider. He is not only physically inferior to the other boys because he is fat, wears glasses, and suffers from "ass-mar" (asthma) (7), but is also socially inferior. Therefore, "lower-middle-class Piggy—with his auntie's sweet shop as signifying the then despised tradesman class, as do the dropped aitches in the lad's speeches—is derided" (Tiger, 30).

Piggy's world is a reasonable one, associated with the rational adult world of science. He declares his philosophy clearly: "Life is scientific, that's what it is" (72). Like a good scientist, Piggy is sensible and clever, able to devise

Piggy (*right*) becomes a scapegoat on the island ruled by the "popular" boys. He is fat, wears glasses, and suffers from asthma, and he is very smart—all traits that make him "suspect" on the good ol' boy island.

schemes to get rescued and to maintain order. He believes that if the boys behave as grown-ups, they will act sensibly for the good of all and that if a ship with grown-ups arrives, the boys will be saved. He becomes disgusted with the other boys when they do irrational things, which he condemns as "[a]cting like a crowd of kids" (30). But the parachutist of the adult world "is dead proof that Piggy's exaggerated respect for adults is itself irrational" (Rosenfield, 131–132).

One of Piggy's greatest failures is his inability to recognize the truth of Simon's belief that the beast is within all people. Instead, he holds the scientific view that "there is no such thing as evil—it is just people behaving irrationally" (McCarron, 4). Although he accurately rejects the idea of an external beast found in the forest or ocean, Piggy inaccurately regards irrational Jack and his tribe as the only evil beings. Since he sees himself as a rational, good person, he refuses to recognize that he also has evil characteristics. Therefore, he will not admit that he participated in Simon's murder, stating, "We never done nothing, we never seen nothing" (140), which is a "last pathetic effort to hang on to the simple view that evil is something done by other people" (Gregor and Kinkead-Weekes, 38). As Friedman makes clear, "[H]is desperate rationalizations point to the inability of human reason to cope with the dark reality of human nature. Piggy's excuses are mere frantic attempts to explain away our basest instincts and actions. Their transparent failure to do so masks the limits of the human intellect" (26).

Piggy's name connects him with the pigs the boys kill and eat. "His physical sloth and appetite and eventual sacrifice" (Oldsey and Weintraub, 32) are all associated with the pigs on the island. Also, like the pigs he is different from the other boys. In fact, Tiger argues that he "is killed because he is alien, a pseudo-species, his death marking the inadequacy of any rational, logical world, for the conch is smashed as a blind Piggy falls into the sea" (Tiger, 47). His death symbolically shows the end of civilization on the tropical island.

Simon

Simon, a name meaning "hearing gladly" in Hebrew (Loughead, 152), is a religious visionary. It was the original name of St. Peter, one of Jesus' chief disciples. The kindest of all the boys, "skinny, vivid little" Simon (24) is gentle and helpful, feeding the littluns fruit and helping build huts. But he is also a strange boy who isolates himself; in fact, the other boys refer to him as "batty" (98). A mystic, Simon is the only one who recognizes that the beast is actually found inside every person, and he is the only one who talks to the Lord of the Flies.

After he encounters the beast's head and recognizes his own capacity for evil, Simon "does what no other boy could dare to do: encounter the beast on the hill" (Tiger, 44). As he releases the dead parachutist, "Simon demonstrates the heroism that has been posited as one side of humankind's dual nature" (Tiger, 45).

Simon is seen as both a prophet and a Christ figure. As a prophet, it is his role to "awaken men to the truth of their own sinfulness" (Boyd, 17), and he therefore attempts to tell the others what he has discovered about the beast. Ironically, the boys see Simon as the beast: "a thing was crawling out of the forest" (136); "The beast stumbled into the horseshoe" (136); "The beast was on his knees" (136); "The beast struggled forward" (136). Therefore, they kill Simon, never recognizing that they, too, are the beast. As Simon tries to bring them knowledge of the truth, "crying out something about a dead man on a hill" (136), the boys stab him to death, thus "re-enacting the crucifixion of Jesus Christ" (Boyd, 17).

Mystic Simon is Golding's mouthpiece for a possible better future for human beings: "What desperate hope the book offers is simply the example of Simon, the acknowledgement of our guilt, of the 'thing of darkness' within us, and the overcoming of this guilt and darkness in generous, if unsuccessful, self-sacrifice for the sake of others" (Boyd, 23).

Roger

Roger, Jack's right-hand man, is a sadist, one who derives pleasure from hurting others. His name means "a Thief-taker," and the term "Old Roger" was a reference to the Devil in the eighteenth century ("Roger," 35). At first Roger's great capacity for evil is not known, because this "slight, furtive boy whom no one knew, who kept to himself with an inner intensity of avoidance and secrecy"(14), is held back from doing evil by his link to civilization. Therefore, as he throws stones at young Henry, he throws to miss while still "enjoying exercising power over him, and flirting pleasurably with the idea of hurting him" (Gregor and Kinkead-Weekes, 17). As time passes and civilization becomes removed, he becomes more sadistic, raping the sow with his spear and killing Piggy with a boulder. After this murder he seems almost ready to overthrow Jack as he "edged past the chief, only just avoiding pushing him with his shoulder" (164). Samneric describe him as "a terror" (171) who is worse than Jack, a fact that seems to be verified when we find out that Roger has "sharpened a stick at both ends" (171) to use for Ralph's severed head. By the end of the novel, "it is not difficult to imagine this sinister figure returning Jack's violent means to power upon him and completing his bloody and Macbeth-like career by sticking *his* head on a pole" (Boyd, 22).

Samneric

The twins, Sam and Eric, so closely united that they are called Samneric, represent mob mentality. Instead of thinking for themselves, they act like ordinary people who follow the crowd, doing good as long as they are part of civilized society but turning evil when they are removed from it. Innocent and friendly, they are loyal to Ralph throughout most of the novel and are "models of decency" like Ralph (Boyd, 20). But they help kill Simon and, unlike Ralph, they deny their actions. After they are forced to join Jack's tribe, "like other ordinary men before them, they have been transformed into concentration camp guards, porters at the Gates of Hell" (Boyd, 20). Worse yet, they betray Ralph and help hunt him down.

British Naval Officer

Although he saves Ralph, the naval officer, who is a warrior and a killer, represents the adult world, which is worse than the boys' society. His life of destruction is masked by his good-looking appearance with his white uniform, gold buttons, and trim cruiser. He expects the boys to portray a similar facade, criticizing them because they did not "put up a better show than that" (182). But as Boyd points out, "the officer is no saviour [*sic*] at all. He is doubly guilty: of being a warrior on behalf of one of the world's two tribes and of sanitizing the killing, the vast butchery, involved in such conflicts, of cleaning and dressing it up so that it seems sane and sensible. He is able to masquerade as a peacemaker, a bringer of light to savages" (Boyd, 13–14).

Symbols

To develop themes, Golding uses several symbols, which are physical objects or characters used to represent abstract ideas.

The Lord of the Flies

The Lord of the Flies, a bloody pig's head that Jack places on a stake as a sacrifice to the beast, is the main symbol of the novel. The words *Lord of the Flies* are a literal translation of the name "Beelzebub," one of the devils in the Bible. However, Golding does not follow the Judeo-Christian beliefs in which an evil Satan fights against a good God. Instead, he shows that evil, the Lord of the Flies, is found only in human beings. Thus, the severed pig's head is not the traditional Beelzebub, because "it does not represent an evil external to the individual, but rather the corrupt and corrupting consciousness, that very human malaise . . . that objectifies evil rather than recognizing its subjectivity" (Tiger, 43). The two representatives of the adult world, the naval officer and Piggy, objectify and distance themselves from evil. For example, Piggy wrongly assumes that evil is caused by things external to them and, therefore, believes that Jack is totally responsible for "things . . . breaking up" (82).

Golding's Lord of the Flies, as several critics point out, is also similar to two Greek gods. It is like Zeus, the king of Olympian gods, who is a god of flies and death (Friedman, 27), and it has even greater similarities to Zeus's son, Dionysus. As dramatized by the ancient Greek writer Euripides in *The Bacchae*, Dionysus is not only the god of wine but also the incarnation of various animals whose primary intention is "to liberate the instinctive life in man from the bondage imposed upon it by reason and social custom" (E. R. Dodds, quoted in Baker, 9). In the play, he comes to Thebes filled with anger against King Pentheus, who, wishing to maintain order in his kingdom, has refused to let his people worship Dionysus. As punishment, Dionysus gets his worshipers to destroy Pentheus's rules, wreck his land, and kill him. Thus, Dionysus is shown "as the source of ecstasies and disasters, as the enemy of intellect and the defense of man against his isolation, as a power that can make him feel like a god while acting like a beast" (R. P. Winnington-Ingram, quoted in Friedman, 14). For the Greeks, resisting Dionysus was disastrous because it meant resisting a central part of a person's own savage inner self. This idea is a main point of Golding's novel. Although the boys attempt to set up a rational, orderly society, they end up with "bloodshed, guilt, utter defeat of reason" (Baker, 9) because the savage, irrational beast, the Lord of the Flies, is a part of every person.

Golding makes it clear that the pig's head is not only the external head of the beast and an offering to the beast, but it is also Simon and, therefore, every person. As Tiger explains, careful parallels are drawn between Simon and the beast. First, their eyes are similar: the pig has "half-shut eyes" (122), while Simon "carefully keep[s] his eyes shut" (123). Second, they both are bloody: the beast's head is "grinning faintly, blood-blackening between the teeth" (122), and the boy's face is filled with blood after "the vessel broke in Simon's nose and the blood gushed out" (129). Third, both Simon and the beast are covered with flies. Initially the flies swarm over the dead pig: the "loudest noise was the buzzing of flies over the spilled guts" (122), but "[a]fter a while these flies found Simon. Gorged, they alighted by his runnels of sweat and drank" (123). It is at this time that Simon realizes his affinity with evil: "At last Simon gave up and looked back; saw the white teeth and dim eyes, the blood—and his gaze was held by the ancient, inescapable recognition" (123). Thus, Simon's head and the beast's head are doubles, and Simon "[l]ooking into the vast mouth, . . . submits to the terror of his own being, . . . [and] penetrate[s] here his own capacity for evil" (Tiger, 44). Golding uses the Lord of the Flies to prove his main theme: that every person has inherent evil.

The Conch

The beautiful conch shell found on the beach by Ralph becomes the symbol of order and democracy. At first the shell is nothing more than a lovely pink-and-cream object that is pulled out of the weeds. It develops a community

THE CONCH, FOUND BY RALPH ON THE BEACH, IS THE SYMBOL OF DEMOCRACY. AS THE BOYS BECOME MORE OUT OF CONTROL, THE SYMBOL IS LITERALLY AND FIGURATIVELY SHATTERED.

purpose after Piggy decides that it should be used as a horn to call the boys together for a meeting. When Ralph attempts to produce a sound out of it, the conch becomes a toy, and he and Piggy enjoy the vulgar noises they produce on it. After the boys assemble, the conch takes on symbolic meaning, becoming identified "with democracy and the right to free speech" (Gregor and Kinkead-Weekes, 4). The boy holding the conch has the authority to speak. In fact, it is partly because Ralph holds the shell that he is elected the leader.

As the boys become savages, the conch loses its symbolic power for the hunters. Ralph, trying desperately to regain order and morality after he helps kill Simon, clings to the conch. But he and Piggy are almost alone in desiring to be good; when they go to Jack's camp and he tries to blow the conch to bring the hunters back to an orderly government, the boys throw stones at him. In the final effort to reestablish a democratic, orderly society, Piggy carries the conch, which "becomes no less than the basic challenge to the Tribe to choose between democracy and anarchy, civilization and savagery" (Gregor and Kinkead-Weekes, 4). The Tribe's answer is almost immediate: "The rock struck Piggy a glancing blow from chin to knee; the conch exploded into a thousand white fragments and ceased to exist" (163). With the conch shattered, Golding symbolically shows that law, order, and democracy on the island cease to exist because most of the boys would sooner do evil than good.

The Signal Fire

The way the boys feel about maintaining a signal fire symbolizes their desire or lack of desire to return to civilization. The first thing Ralph asks the boys to do is to make a fire to alert a passing ship so that they can be rescued. Since they want to go back home, all of them rush to the mountain to gather wood and build a fire. Jack and his choir volunteer to maintain the fire at all times. But before long, the choirboys prefer hunting to fire building. When Jack lets the fire go out, Golding shows that they no longer wish to return to civilization but would sooner remain on the island as savages. Although Ralph tries to keep the fire going because he feels that "[t]he fire is the most important thing on the island" and tells the boys that "we ought to—ought to die before we let the fire out" (69), he does not have enough people left in his tribe to succeed.

Ironically, the fire that attracts the notice of the ship at the end of the novel is not a signal fire but a fire set to destroy the island's vegetation so Jack and his savage tribe can find and kill Ralph.

Piggy's Glasses

Intelligent, rational Piggy is the only boy who wears glasses, which symbolize the scientific, rational views admired and accepted by society. At the beginning of the novel, the boys rationally use Piggy's glasses to focus the heat of the sun to make a rescue fire. Later, when Jack, angry that Ralph blames him for letting the signal fire go out, strikes out at Piggy and breaks one of the lenses of the glasses, Golding symbolically shows that reason has begun to lose its power over the boys. They would rather spend their time destroying the lives of pigs than keeping a fire going. The rational world is totally destroyed when Jack and his hunters steal Piggy's glasses; Ralph's small group has lost all of its influence and power. Order and reason are gone.

The Characters as Allegorical Figures

Ever since *Lord of the Flies* was first published, critics have recognized that the novel is a type of allegory whose characters represent ideas or themes. However, because "Golding is a simply complicated writer" (Oldsey and Weintraub, 28), the characters are not straightforward representations of only one idea. They can represent various categories of allegories—political, sociological, religious, and psychological.

Read as a political novel in which two types of governments struggle for supremacy, "Jack may appear to be the demagogic dictator and Roger his sadistic henchman; Ralph may be a confused democrat, with Piggy his 'brain trust'" (Oldsey and Weintraub, 29). The littluns are the common people, while the older boys are the ruling classes. The good boys—Ralph, Piggy, and Simon—use their authority to help and protect the little boys and to do things for the benefit of society, while evil Jack and Roger exert their power to fulfill their own lusts and desires.

As a social allegory, the novel describes "the way in which, when the civilized restraints which we impose on ourselves are abandoned, the passions of anger, lust and fear wash across the mind, obliterating commonsense and care, and life once again becomes nasty, brutish and short" (Bowden, 54). On the side of civilization are Ralph, symbolizing leadership, law, and order; Piggy, representing the rational, scientific, intellectual aspects of civilization; and Simon, representing human goodness. On the side of savage cruelty are Jack, symbolizing bloodthirstiness, savagery, and lust for power; and Roger, showing savagery in its greatest form.

The novel can also be read as a religious allegory in which the story of the fall of humankind is told. The island, like the Garden of Eden in the Bible, becomes a fiery hell at the end of the novel, set ablaze by Jack, who is like the chief devil, Satan, the destroyer of humankind, and his team of devils. They pursue Ralph, the boy who represents the first human being, Adam, whom Satan tempted to sin so that he would go to hell. They have already killed "Piggy, the 'sage' who is blind without his glasses, . . . and 'sacrifice[d]' Simon, the only one among them who has gone up to the top of the mountain and discovered the truth" (Bowden, 54).

Psychological critics also view the novel as an allegory of evil, but they follow Freud's theory that gods and devils are "nothing other than psychological processes projected unto the outer world" (quoted in Jones, 53). These critics see Jack as the id, "an externalization of the evil instinctual forces of the unconscious"; Ralph as the ego, "a projection of man's good impulses from which we derive authority figures"; and Piggy as the superego, "man's reasoning faculties" (Rosenfield, 122–123). The boys on the island become more and more irrational, mimicking what Golding regarded as the great adult irrational act: war.

All of these allegorical interpretations have some flaws, because they do not perfectly explain every character, nor do they provide an explicit moral. Therefore, some critics suggest that it is best to see this allegorical novel as "rich in variant suggestions" (Oldsey and Weintraub, 31).

Motifs

To help develop his themes, Golding uses motifs, which are recurring structures, phrases, or literary devices.

Ballantyne's Novel, *The Coral Island*

The central motif of *Lord of the Flies* is Robert Michael Ballantyne's 1857 novel, *The Coral Island*, which Golding uses to contrast "two radically different pictures of human nature and society" (Baker, 4). In Ballantyne's novel, British boys abandoned on an island follow three reasonable leaders who create an idyllic society, defeat fierce pirates, and convert cannibalistic savages to Christianity. Ballantyne, therefore, portrays man as inherently good while evil is an external force found in the pirates and savages. Golding's boys, like Ballantyne's, are marooned on a tropical island; his characters are similar, too. In fact, two, Ralph and Jack, have the same names as

Ballantyne's, although Golding splits Ballantyne's third leader, Peterkin, into two boys, Piggy and Simon.

To make sure that readers compare the two novels, Golding mentions Ballantyne's novel by name at the beginning and the end of the novel. When he first arrives, Ralph notes that the island is "a coral island" (8), and after he calls the boys together, he points out that the island has "a coral reef" (21). Jack, Ralph, and Simon proclaim that it is "a good island" similar to those described in romance and adventure books they have read, such as *Treasure Island* and *Coral Island* (26). They expect that their stay here will be similar to the one experienced in *The Coral Island*. But, of course, Golding's boys have a far different experience from the one found in Ballantyne's novel. At the very end of *Lord of the Flies*, Ballantyne's novel is again referred to, this time by the naval officer who rescues the boys. As he surveys the situation, he says, "Jolly good show. Like the Coral Island" (182), as he mistakes the boys' hunt to kill Ralph for fun and games. His statement thus shows his naivety about the evil nature of human beings. Ralph, on the other hand, cannot return to the false optimism of the officer or the false premises of *The Coral Island*.

Having "Fun"

Four times in the novel, someone talks about "having fun," forcing readers to reconsider these words that initially seem innocent. The first time, the words are spoken by Ralph as he informs the others about the "good island" and declares that "[u]ntil the grownups come to fetch us we'll have fun" (27). He expects they will have a series of adventures, live an idyllic life on the island, and eventually get rescued. Ralph, then, "tells the boys what mankind has always wished to hear: that there is no troublesome competition among our desires, that the world will complaisantly minister to all our wishes, that fun and rescue fit easily into one package" (Reilly, 112).

However, when Beelzebub says, "We are going to have fun on this island!" (144), he means something entirely different. His method of having fun is to see what evil will manifest itself in the boys when all constraints are removed and they are free to unleash their savage inner beings. Beelzebub's fun is seen through Jack, who asks, "Who'll join my tribe and have fun?" (134). That night, the boys kill Simon.

At the end of the novel, the uncomprehending rescuer, looking at the painted bodies of little boys carrying sharp sticks, naively repeats Ralph's sentiments at the beginning of the book. He mutters, "Fun and games" and "grinned cheerfully at Ralph" (181). Although the adult does not understand, Ralph now knows the horrible truth about human nature.

Repeated Actions

Golding uses a number of repeated actions "to create a vague yet familiar threat, a sense of doom which cannot be adequately located in the narrative's thrust until its confirmation in the coda" (Tiger, 36). Each action starts as an innocent deed and ends as an act of great evil. The boys roll larger and larger stones until Piggy is destroyed by a boulder, and Ralph is flushed out of hiding by a rock "that was half as big as a cottage, big as a car, a tank" (174). Three bodies are swept out to sea—the dead parachutist, whose body terrified the boys; Simon, who is killed because of the boys' fear of a beast; and Piggy, who is savagely murdered. The boys turn cartwheels at various times to express their happiness, beginning with Ralph, who is elated that the island is good, and ending with Jack and his tribe after they steal Piggy's glasses, ensuring that Jack now has total power. Ralph runs two races. He first tears up the mountain to reset the signal fire that has gone out, showing his desire to get rescued and return to civilization; he runs the second race to escape death as he is pursued by all the other boys. Twice Roger "sharpened a stick at both ends" (121, 171); the first stick was for a pig's head and the second for Ralph's. There are three hunts described in detail. In the beginning, Jack has too much respect for life to kill a pig. But soon he resorts to torturing a sow before he kills it, severs its head, and places it on a stick. In the last hunt, Ralph has replaced the pig as the boys try to force him out of hiding so they can cut off his head and place it on a stick. "These sequences of repeated actions, placed at intervals during the story, intensify the ambiguous threat and give the illusion of a vastly speeded-up denouement" (Tiger, 36).

Literary Reception of the Novel

When *Lord of the Flies* was published in Great Britain in 1954, it met with mostly positive reviews. For example, Douglas Hewitt, writing for *The Manchester Guardian*, found it a "magnificent" work that was "completely convincing and often very frightening" (4); James Stern in the *New York Times Book Review* declared it was a "highly original," "superbly written, brilliant work" (6–7); and Dan Wickenden in the *New York Herald Tribune Weekly Book Review* proclaimed it "an exciting and ultimately powerful narrative" and overall "a distinguished performance" (9). However, some reviewers were not as enthusiastic. British critic Walter Allen in the *New Statesman* described the novel as a "skillfully told" story but "rather unpleasant and too easily affecting" (3). Louis J. Halle's disapproval in the *Saturday Review* was stronger; he argued that Golding's vision as a novelist conflicted with his ideas as a social scientist, leaving the reader with a book that was "the dead stick of an academic conception" (6).

Although reviews were mixed, the novel sold well in England, but in the United States, the book sold "only 2,383 copies, and quickly went out of print" (*Time*, 141).

However, some academic critics were impressed with the work and recommended it to their students. Therefore, when the paperback edition was issued in 1959, it was very successful in America, rivaling J. D. Salinger's *The Catcher in the Rye* as the favorite novel on college campuses. By the early 1960s the book was recognized as "the most important novel to be published in this country in the 1950s" (Cox, 82–83), and Golding was proclaimed "the most important practicing novelist in English" (Kermode, 107). By 1962 the book was so profitable that Golding was able to quit teaching and spend his time at home writing.

Even though the novel has been highly praised throughout the decades, it has also been heavily criticized. The major criticism revolves around the character of Simon, who is "the cause of the most serious rift among the critics, the rock indeed upon which much opinion founders" (Reilly, 117). Virginia Tiger explains that "Simon's symbolic function in the novel as the agent who provides the text's fabular message—that 'mankind is both heroic and sick'—has provoked the greatest negative criticism over the years, underscoring the charge that *Lord of the Fires* was thesis-ridden, facile in its didactic intent, an over-schematic allegory whose rhetorical effects were too rigidly patterned" (31–32). Harold Bloom's criticism, that "saintly Simon strains credibility as a naturalistic portrait" (5), is a typical charge leveled against Golding's novel. Critics have described Simon as "the one weakness in the book" (Cox, 87), a character who is "neither plausible nor representative" because he is "constantly weakened by Golding's attempt to endow him with a mysterious authority and insight" (Walters, 100). However, others argue that the character of Simon is "the most original . . . creation in *Lord of the Flies*" (Reilly, 117).

The general public has also objected to Golding's novel; in fact, censors have tried to remove it from libraries and schools a number of times. It was first challenged in 1974 at the Dallas, Texas, Independent School District high school libraries. In the 1980s more challenges appeared. In 1981 Owen, North Carolina, High School objected to the book because it was "demoralizing inasmuch as it implies that man is little more than an animal." In 1984 the Olney, Texas, Independent School District wanted it banned because of "excessive violence and bad language." And in 1988 the board of education in Toronto, Canada, ruled that Golding's book was "racist and recommended that it be removed from all schools" after "parents and members of the black community complained about a reference to 'niggers' in the book and said it denigrates blacks." Sully Buttes, South Dakota, High School in 1981 and Marana, Arizona, High School in 1983 also challenged this book. In the next decade, people in Waterloo, Iowa, objected to the book because of its "profanity, lurid passages about sex, and statements defamatory to minorities, God, women and the disabled." As recently as 2000, people in Bloomfield, New York, wanted it removed from the ninth-grade accelerated English reading list (Doyle, no. 517).

In spite of these objections, *Lord of the Flies* has been popular for almost sixty years. It has been "a huge international success and has now been translated into twenty-six languages and sold millions of copies" (McCarron, 2). It continues to appeal to readers for two primary reasons. First, as a narrative, Golding's novel is "exceptionally exciting and moving" (Drew, 10). Second, readers admire the complexity and deeper significance of Golding's book: "They are drawn to Golding to question reflectively, to try to answer and to know" (Fuller, 145).

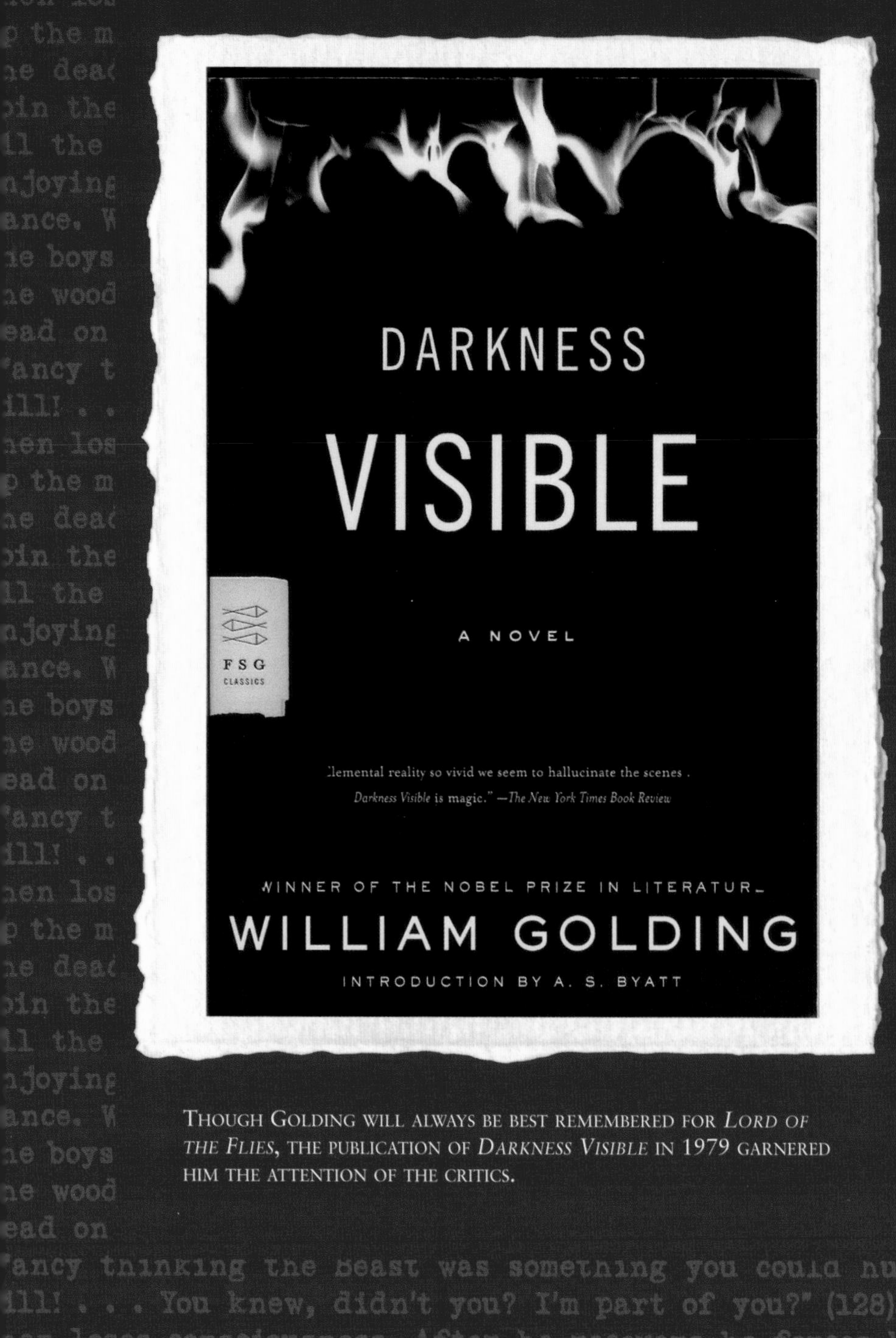

THOUGH GOLDING WILL ALWAYS BE BEST REMEMBERED FOR *LORD OF THE FLIES*, THE PUBLICATION OF *DARKNESS VISIBLE* IN 1979 GARNERED HIM THE ATTENTION OF THE CRITICS.

Chapter 4

Golding's Place in Literature

WILLIAM GOLDING attained international recognition and critical acclaim after he published his first novel, *Lord of the Flies*, in 1954. The initial reviews of the book were mostly enthusiastic, as critics "praised Golding's fine writing," although some found "the metaphor too neat, too explicit, too heavy, or too limited—in one way or another, inadequate to suggest anything important or interesting about contemporary British society or the human condition" (Gindin, 89). After Golding published his next books, *The Inheritors* in 1955 and *Pincher Martin* in 1956, reviewers began to look at him as a serious novelist. For the most part, their reactions were positive. For example, the *New Statesman* in 1958 called Golding "the most original of our contemporaries" and praised him as "a writer of intense visual gift, with an overpowering sense of nature and an extraordinary perception of man as a physical being in a physical world, torn between a primitive inheritance and the glimmer of an evolving mind" (Pritchett, 36). Of these early books, reviewers generally felt that *Lord of the Flies* was "the most accomplished of Mr. Golding's novels" (Pritchett, 38).

Not everyone praised Golding, especially after the publication of *Free Fall* in 1959. In fact, the *Nation* did not think that Golding's "considerable, but unofficial, reputation in the country" was deserved. Although it noted that many critics claimed that "he is the most original and profound of the postwar novelists in Britain" because he is able "to make brilliant use of *symbolism*, to deploy the findings of modern thought about *man-in-society*, to have a vision of the *evil* inherent in human nature," it declared in 1960 that "Golding is not importantly original in thought or feeling," and "he is not a significant artist" because "[t]here is no life in his language; it is all ingenuity, intention and synthetics" (Martin Green, 75–79).

In spite of some skeptical critics, Golding gained popular and academic admiration during the 1950s and early 1960s. Teachers assigned *Lord of the Flies* in introductory university and college classes; it "was required reading for students in political science, used to illustrate the anti-pastoral, and assigned to Peace Corps volunteers to learn 'about the essential conflict between man's individual well being and the rules of society'" (quoted in Dick, 97). Soon college readers embraced *Lord of the Flies* as enthusiastically as they had J. D. Salinger's *The Catcher in the Rye* a decade earlier, and Golding became a campus cult figure. Golding's reputation as a strong, imaginative novelist was so great that *Time* proclaimed him "Lord of the Campus" (141).

With the publication of *The Spire* in 1964, Golding's critical approval began to crumble, a "critical eclipse, which lasted for the rest of the 1960s, and much of the 1970s" (Doering, 287). One radio reviewer so strongly disapproved of *The Spire* that he "suggested that it be viewed as a companion piece to the work of the Brontë sisters, under a new title—'Wuthering Depths'" (quoted in Doering, 286). Golding's next book, a collection of essays called *The Hot Gates, and Other Occasional Pieces*, published in 1965, was not warmly received. And his books of fiction—*The Pyramid*, which appeared in 1967, and *The Scorpion God*, which came out in 1971—were censured because they were short stories rather than novels. Throughout the rest of the 1970s Golding published nothing, and few critics took note of him.

However, after eight years of silence, Golding once again gained critical attention with the publication of

Darkness Visible in 1979. When he followed it with *Rites of Passage* a year later, he received more recognition. Each novel was awarded a prestigious national literary award. These novels made Golding once again a popular figure in Britain. After he published his second book of essays, *A Moving Target*, in 1982, Golding received universal acclamation when he was awarded the most prestigious literary award, the Nobel Prize in Literature, in 1983. Although some people criticized the Nobel judges for choosing Golding, many agreed with James Gindin that Golding "fully deserve[d] . . . the public recognition that the award of the Nobel Prize suggests" (111).

Golding continued to produce books throughout the 1980s: three novels—*The Paper Men* (1984), *Close Quarters* (1987), and *Fire Down Below* (1989)—and a travelogue, *An Egyptian Journal* (1985). After his death in

In 1983, Golding received the Nobel Prize in Literature. He continued to publish fiction and nonfiction until shortly before he died.

1993, Golding's final novel, *The Double Tongue*, appeared in 1995. Although all of these works were noticed and reviewed, none achieved the critical or popular acclaim of *Lord of the Flies*.

In spite of not having the enthusiastic approval of the critics, Golding was recognized as a leading British writer from the mid–1960s until his death. In acknowledgment of his achievements, he received honorary degrees from the Universities of Sussex (1970), Kent (1974), Warwick (1981), Oxford (1983), the Sorbonne in Paris (1983), Bristol (1984), and Oviedo in Spain (1991). The British government also recognized his accomplishments, making him Commander of the Order of the British Empire in 1965 and knighting him in 1988.

Throughout his life and to the present time, Golding's popularity has been almost totally dependent on *Lord of the Flies*. In 2003, it was voted one of Britain's one hundred best-loved novels by the public as part of the BBC's "The Big Read." The novel has been translated into a number of languages, and twice it has been made into a movie. Peter Brook's 1963 version, filmed by British Lion Films from Golding's screenplay, closely follows the original text and has British schoolboys stranded on an island, while the 1990 Hollywood film by Castle Rock Entertainment uses American military cadets. *Lord of the Flies* has also been made into a play by Nigel Williams.

Many authors have borrowed elements from the plot of *Lord of the Flies*. In 1955, only a year after its publication, Robert A. Heinlein refuted Golding's ideas in *Tunnel in the Sky* by having his teenagers, who are stranded on an uninhabited planet, create a workable society. A DC Comics series, *Salvation Run*, employed a similar plot, having all the major villains marooned on an alien planet. Additional aspects of *Lord of the Flies* have been used by other writers. For instance, Stephen King featured Golding's book in both *Cujo* in 1981 and *Hearts in Atlantis* in 1999, and he adopted Golding's term "Castle Rock" as the name of a town in several of his novels. Rob Reiner, who liked the name of King's town, named his production company Castle Rock Entertainment, which, incidentally, was the company that produced the 1990 film of *Lord of the Flies*.

Other media have also been inspired by Golding's novel. In television, Sunrise Animation's series *Infinite Ryvius* relied on Golding's plot as it told the stories of different teenagers who were marooned on a space battleship; *The Simpsons* had an episode, "Das Bus," based on Golding's novel; and *Spongebob Squarepants*, in "The Club Spongebob" episode, used a magic conch. Musicians, too, have incorporated elements of *Lord of the Flies* in their works. The English heavy metal band Iron Maiden wrote a song about Golding's novel, titling it "Lord of the Flies"; and the Irish rock band U2 composed another called "Shadows and Tall Trees," taking its title from Golding's chapter with the same name.

The novel is so well known that the words *Lord of the Flies* have entered contemporary culture as shorthand for any instance of a descent into group savagery.

Although *Lord of the Flies* remains popular with the media and with readers, few literary critics have analyzed any of Golding's books in recent years. In 1988 James Gindin noted that Golding "remains on the fringes of literary discussion and concern" (111), a shift that began in the early 1980s and continues today. Jonathan W. Doering offered an explanation for this lack of enthusiasm, explaining that Golding did not write the types of books the commentators expected him to produce because he "refused to confine himself to one topical hinterland, to one implied audience" (290). Instead, Golding wrote books in a variety of styles, structures, and narrative techniques; and he constantly chose new subjects: "desert islands; the dawn of humanity; the Second World War, both at land and at sea; the medieval English Church; early twentieth century English country life; the Ancient World (Egypt, Rome, Africa); a nineteenth century ship of the line; a meditation on good and evil in modern Britain; a contemporary novelist's headlong flight from academic mummification; and the Temple of Apollo at Delphi" (Doering, 286). Those critics who do discuss Golding's works are divided into two groups concerning his place in literature: one group disparages him as a limited writer who talks about a single idea, the evil of humans, while the other side considers him one of the finest British novelists of the twentieth century whose international reputation is well earned.

No matter how people view him critically, they cannot deny that he is among the most well-liked and influential British authors since World War II. The Nobel Prize committee accurately summed up the reasons for Golding's popularity: "William Golding's novels and stories are . . . not only somber moralities and dark myths about evil and treacherous destructive forces . . . they are also colourful tales of adventure which can be read as such, full of narrative joy, inventiveness, and excitement" (quoted in Doering, 288).

Works

Novels and Stories

1954 *Lord of the Flies*
1955 *The Inheritors*
1956 "Envoy Extraordinary"; published in *Sometime, Never: Three Tales of Imagination*, by Golding, John Wyndham, and Mervyn Peake
1956 *Pincher Martin*; also published as *The Two Deaths of Christopher Martin* in 1957
1959 *Free Fall*
1964 *The Spire*
1967 *The Pyramid*
1971 *The Scorpion God: Three Short Novels*; comprised of "Envoy Extraordinary," "Clonk Clonk," and "The Scorpion God"
1979 *Darkness Visible*
1980 *Rites of Passage*
1984 *The Paper Men*
1987 *Close Quarters*
1989 *Fire Down Below*
1991 *To the Ends of the Earth: A Sea Trilogy*; comprised of *Rites of Passage*, *Close Quarters*, and *Fire Down Below*
1995 *The Double Tongue*

Poetry

1934 *Poems*

Essays and Lectures

1965 *The Hot Gates, and Other Occasional Pieces*
1982 *A Moving Target*

1984 *Nobel Lecture, 7 December 1983*
1985 *An Egyptian Journal*

Plays

1958 *The Brass Butterfly: A Play in Three Acts*; an adaptation of "Envoy Extraordinary"

Produced Radio Scripts

1956 "Our Way of Life," BBC
1960 "Miss Pulkinhorn," BBC
1961 "Break My Heart," BBC

Other Works

1963 *Lord of the Flies*, screenplay by Golding, British Lion Films
1970 "Foreword," in T*alk: Conversations with William Golding* by Jack Biles
1988 "Miss Pulkinhorn," in *The Penguin Book of Modern British Short Stories*, edited by Malcolm Bradbury
1994 "Foreword," in *William Golding: A Bibliography 1934–1993*, edited by R. A. Gekoski and P. A. Grogan

Selected Periodical Publications—Essays, Reviews, Short Stories

1957 "The Writer in His Age," *London Magazine*, 4 May
"Children's Books: Senior Bookshelf," *Listener*, December
1958 "Pincher Martin," *Radio Times*, 21 March
1959 "The Anglo-Saxon," *Queen*, 22 December
1960 "The Ladder and the Tree," *Listener*, 24 March
"In Retreat," review of *A Hermit Disclosed* by Raleigh Trevelyan, *Spectator*, 25 March
"Raider," review of *John Paul Jones* by Samuel Eliot Morrison, *Spectator*, 20 May

"Islands," *Spectator*, 10 June
"On the Crest of the Wave," *Times Literary Supplement*, 17 June
"Miss Pulkinhorn," *Encounter*, August
"Headmasters," *Spectator*, 12 August
"In My Ark," *Spectator*, 16 September
"Man of God," review of *The Sabres of Paradise* by Leslie Blanch, *Spectator*, 7 October
"Prospect of Eton," review of *Eton* by Christopher Hollis, *Spectator*, 25 November
"Billy the Kid," *Spectator*, 25 November

1961 "Thin Partitions," review of *Some Reflections on Genius and Other Essays* by Russell Brain, *Spectator*, 13 January
"The Rise of Love," review of *The Characters of Love* by John Bayley, *Spectator*, 10 February
"Androids All," review of *New Maps of Hell* by Kingsley Amis, *Spectator*, 24 February
"All or Nothing," review of *The Faithful Thinker*, edited by A. C. Harwood, *Spectator*, 24 March
"Before the Beginning," review of *World Prehistory* by Grahame Clark, *Spectator*, 26 May
"Astronaut by Gaslight," *Spectator*, 9 June
"It's a Long Way to Oxyrhynchus," *Spectator*, 7 July
"Thinking as a Hobby," *Holiday*, August
"Tolstoy's Mountain," *Spectator*, 8 September
"A Touch of Insomnia," *Spectator*, 27 October
"The Glass Door," *Spectator*, 24 November
"The English Channel," *Holiday*, November

1962 "Body and Soul," *Spectator*, 19 January
"Shakespeare's Birthplace," *Holiday*, May
"Gradus ad Parnassum," *Spectator*, 7 September
"Surge and Thunder," *Spectator*, 14 September

1963 "Digging for Pictures," *Holiday*, March

	"Exile, Poverty, Homecoming," *Holiday*, April
	"Advice to a Nervous Visitor," *Holiday*, July
1964	"The Best of Luck," *Holiday*, May
1965	"The Condition of the Novel," *New Left Review*, January–February
1966	"Egypt and I," *Holiday*, April
	"Inside a Pyramid," *Esquire*, 19 December
1967	"On the Escarpment," *Kenyon*, June
	"Delphi: The Oracle Revealed," *Holiday*, August

Filmography

Films of Novels

Lord of the Flies. Film. Dir. Harry Hook. Castle Rock Entertainment/MGM. 1990.

Lord of the Flies. Film. Dir. Peter Brook. Two Arts Ltd. 1963.

The Spire. Film. Dir. Roger Spottiswoode. Picture Palace. 2008.

To the Ends of the Earth, 3-part TV series. Dir. David Attwood. BBC. 2005.

Films on Golding and His Works

William Golding: "Lord of the Flies." Films for the Humanities & Sciences. 1999.

Lord of the Flies. Dir. Edward James Olmos. Films for the Humanities & Sciences. 1998.

"William Golding," *Great Writers of the 20th Century*. Film series. BBC. 1996.

ad on the stake. It becomes the Lord of the Flies, say-
cy thinking the Beast was something you could hunt and
You knew, didn't you? I'm part of you?" (128). Simon then
sciousness. After he recovers he forces himself up the
to discover the nature of the "beast" and finds the dead
st, whom he releases. He then attempts to join the oth-
ll them about his discovery. Meanwhile, all the boys,
Ralph and Piggy, are in Jack's camp enjoying the pig
participating in the pig-killing dance. When Simon
into the camp during the dance, the boys beat him to
inking he is the beast. Alone in the woods next to the
g's head, Simon listens to the head on the stake. It
he Lord of the Flies, saying, "Fancy thinking the Beast
hing you could hunt and kill! . . . You knew, didn't you?
f you?" (128). Simon then loses consciousness. After he
he forces himself up the mountain to discover the nature
ast" and finds the dead parachutist, whom he releases.
ttempts to join the others to tell them about his dis-
anwhile, all the boys, including Ralph and Piggy, are
camp enjoying the pig feast and participating in the
g dance. When Simon stumbles into the camp during the
boys beat him to death, thinking he is the beast. Alone
ods next to the bloody pig's head, Simon listens to the
the stake. It becomes the Lord of the Flies, saying,
nking the Beast was something you could hunt and kill!
new, didn't you? I'm part of you?" (128). Simon then loses
ness. After he recovers he forces himself up the moun-
iscover the nature of the "beast" and finds the dead
st, whom he releases. He then attempts to join the oth-
ll them about his discovery. Meanwhile, all the boys,
Ralph and Piggy, are in Jack's camp enjoying the pig
participating in the pig-killing dance. When Simon
into the camp during the dance, the boys beat him to
inking he is the beast. Alone in the woods next to the
g's head, Simon listens to the head on the stake. It
he Lord of the Flies, saying, "Fancy thinking the Beast
hing you could hunt and kill! . . . You knew, didn't you?
f you?" (128). Simon then loses consciousness. After he
he forces himself up the mountain to discover the nature
ast" and finds the dead parachutist, whom he releases.
ttempts to join the others to tell them about his dis-
anwhile, all the boys, including Ralph and Piggy, are

Chronology

1911	
September 19:	William Gerald Golding is born at Karenza, Newquay, in Cornwall, England, the second son of Alec and Mildred Golding.
1919:	Begins dame school.
1921–1930:	Attends Marlborough Grammar School in Wiltshire, where his father is science master.
1930:	Enters Brasenose College, Oxford, to read Natural Sciences.
1932:	Changes his studies to English literature.
1934	
June:	Gains a B.A. honors degree in English from Brasenoe College.
Autumn:	*Poems*, Golding's first book, is published by Macmillan.
1934–1935:	Gains theatrical training and experience at the Little Theatre in Hampstead and at the Citizen's Theatre in Bath.
1935	
Autumn:	Becomes a teacher at Michael Hall in South London, staying there two years.

1937:	Goes back to Oxford to study for a teaching qualification.
1938	
January:	Starts his teaching practice at Bishop Wordsworth's School, Salisbury.
June:	Receives his teaching diploma.
September:	Takes a post at Maidstone Grammar School. Meets Ann Brookfield, and they fall in love.
1939	
September:	Marries Ann Brookfield in Maidstone Registry Office.
1940	
April:	Becomes a schoolmaster at Bishop Wordsworth's School in Salisbury; moves into a cottage in the Wiltshire village of Bowerchalke with his wife.
September:	The Golding's first child, David, is born.
December:	Leaves Bishop Wordsworth's School to join the Royal Navy.
1941–1945:	Serves in World War II. His first active service is on HMS *Galatea* in the North Atlantic Ocean. He then goes to Liverpool, where he works as a guard in the Gladstone Dock. In spring 1942, he works at a weapons research unit in Buckinghamshire. In early 1943, he requests to return to active duty at sea. He is sent to New York to help bring minesweepers back to the UK. Later, he is trained in landing crafts equipped with rocket guns. He commands this type of vessel and takes part in the naval support for the D-day landings in 1944 and the invasion of Walcheren in 1945.

1945
July: The Goldings' second and last child, Judith Diana, is born.
September: Leaves the navy and returns to Bishop Wordsworth's School, where he teaches until 1961.
1946: The Goldings move to Salisbury.

1947–1952: Writes several novels that are rejected by publishers.

1952: Begins working on a novel he calls *Strangers from Within.*

1953: Submits *Strangers from Within* to publishers. Many reject it before he sends it to Faber and Faber in September, where it is accepted.

1954
September: Novel is published with a new title, *Lord of the Flies.*

1955
September: *The Inheritors* is published.
Golding is made a Fellow of the Royal Society of Literature.

1956
August: The Goldings travel to France in their new boat, *Wild Rose.*
October: Novel *Pincher Martin* is published.
"Envoy Extraordinary" is published in a volume of three stories, *Sometime, Never: Three Tales of Imagination.* The other two stories are written by John Wyndham and Mervyn Peake.

1957:	Writes for *The Bookman* and *The Listener*, and begins broadcasting. *Pincher Martin* is published in the United States as *The Two Deaths of Christopher Martin*.
1958	
February 24:	*The Brass Butterfly: A Play in Three Acts*, adapted from "Envoy Extraordinary," opens in Oxford, tours the provinces, and runs for a month in London.
July:	The text of the play is published.
Autumn:	The Goldings move back to the village of Bowerchalke.
November:	Golding's father, Alec Golding, is diagnosed with cancer.
December 12:	Alec Golding dies suddenly of a heart attack.
1959	
October:	*Free Fall* is published.
1960:	Publishes a number of short works.
August:	Golding's mother, Mildred Golding, dies.
1961	
April:	The Goldings and their children travel to Greece.
Autumn:	Lives in the United States with his wife, where Golding is a writer in residence at Hollins College in Virginia.
1962:	Publishes six items in periodicals. Resigns from Bishop Wordsworth's School and becomes a full-time writer.
1963	
May:	*Lord of the Flies* is made into a film, directed by Peter Brook.
1964	
April:	*The Spire* is published.
Summer:	The Golding family lives in Greece.

1965:	*The Hot Gates, and Other Occasional Pieces*, Golding's first book of essays, is published.
December:	*The Brass Butterfly* is performed at Lincoln Center in New York.
1966:	Is made a Commander of the Order of the British Empire (CBE). Becomes an honorary fellow of Brasenose College, Oxford. Buys a new sailing boat, *Tenace*, with his wife.
1967	
June:	*The Pyramid* is published.
July:	The *Tenace* is run down and sinks off the Isle of Wight.
1970:	Is awarded an honorary doctor of letters (D.Litt.) by the University of Sussex.
1971	
Autumn:	Begins keeping a journal of his attempts to write and his personal experiences.
October:	*The Scorpion God: Three Short Novels* is published. It contains "Envoy Extraordinary" and two other stories.
1974:	The University of Kent makes Golding an honorary D.Litt.
1976:	Travels to Egypt with his wife.
1979	
October:	*Darkness Visible* is published, winning the James Tait Black Memorial Prize for Fiction Best Novel.
1980	
October:	*Rites of Passage* is published, winning the Booker McConnell Prize as the year's best novel.
1981:	The University of Warwick makes Golding an honorary D.Litt.

1982: *A Moving Target*, Golding's second book of essays, is published.

1983
Summer: Both Oxford University and the Sorbonne give Golding honorary doctorates.
October: Golding receives the Nobel Prize for Literature.

1984
February: *The Paper Men* is published.
Spring: Visits Egypt with his wife.
Summer: The University of Bristol makes Golding an honorary LLD.

1985
April: The Goldings move to Cornwall.
July: *An Egyptian Journal*, a record of Golding's travels in Egypt, is published.

1986: Faber and Faber publishes *William Golding: The Man and his Books, A Tribute on his 75th Birthday*, edited by John Carey.

1987
June: *Close Quarters*, a sequel to *Rites of Passage*, is published.

1988: Is made Knight of the British Empire.

1989
March: *Fire Down Below*, a sequel to *Close Quarters* and the final novel of the Sea Trilogy, is published.

1990: A new film version of *Lord of the Flies* appears, with American schoolboys replacing the English originals.

1991:	*To the Ends of the Earth: A Sea Trilogy* is published.
1992:	Works on "Scenes from a Life."
Summer:	Is awarded an honorary D.Litt. by the University of Oviedo in Spain.
Autumn:	Is diagnosed with a malignant melanoma on his face.
December:	The melanoma is removed.
1993	
January:	Begins writing a new novel.
June 19:	Dies in Cornwall, England, of heart failure.
June 24:	Is buried in the churchyard at Bowerchalke.
November:	Is remembered at a memorial service in Salisbury Cathedral.
1995	
January 1:	Ann Brookfield Golding dies.
June:	Golding's last novel, *The Double Tongue*, is published.

ad on the stake. It becomes the Lord of the Flies, say-
y thinking the Beast was something you could hunt and
You knew, didn't you? I'm part of you?" (128). Simon then
ciousness. After he recovers he forces himself up the
to discover the nature of the "beast" and finds the dead
st, whom he releases. He then attempts to join the oth-
l them about his discovery. Meanwhile, all the boys,
Ralph and Piggy, are in Jack's camp enjoying the pig
participating in the pig-killing dance. When Simon
into the camp during the dance, the boys beat him to
inking he is the beast. Alone in the woods next to the
g's head, Simon listens to the head on the stake. It
e Lord of the Flies, saying, "Fancy thinking the Beast
ing you could hunt and kill! . . . You knew, didn't you?
f you?" (128). Simon then loses consciousness. After he
e forces himself up the mountain to discover the nature
ast" and finds the dead parachutist, whom he releases.
ttempts to join the others to tell them about his dis-
anwhile, all the boys, including Ralph and Piggy, are
camp enjoying the pig feast and participating in the
g dance. When Simon stumbles into the camp during the
boys beat him to death, thinking he is the beast. Alone
ods next to the bloody pig's head, Simon listens to the
he stake. It becomes the Lord of the Flies, saying,
nking the Beast was something you could hunt and kill!
new, didn't you? I'm part of you?" (128). Simon then loses
ess. After he recovers he forces himself up the moun-
iscover the nature of the "beast" and finds the dead
st, whom he releases. He then attempts to join the oth-
l them about his discovery. Meanwhile, all the boys,
Ralph and Piggy, are in Jack's camp enjoying the pig
participating in the pig-killing dance. When Simon
nto the camp during the dance, the boys beat him to
nking he is the beast. Alone in the woods next to the
's head, Simon listens to the head on the stake. It
e Lord of the Flies, saying, "Fancy thinking the Beast
ing you could hunt and kill! . . . You knew, didn't you?
f you?" (128). Simon then loses consciousness. After he
e forces himself up the mountain to discover the nature
ast" and finds the dead parachutist, whom he releases.
ttempts to join the others to tell them about his dis-
anwhile, all the boys, including Ralph and Piggy, are

Notes

Chapter 1

p. 9, par. 2, Aspects of Golding's life are found in the interviews he granted; the articles published by his daughter, friends, and acquaintances; and the essays he wrote, particularly those in *The Hot Gates* and *A Moving Target*. Two of his essays are autobiographical: "Billy the Kid" and "The Ladder and the Tree," both published in *The Hot Gates*. His other autobiographical essay, "Scenes from a Life," was published after his death.

p. 15, par 2, Golding said about the novels of Jules Verne: "[They] held me rapt, I dived with the *Nautilus*, was shot round the moon, crossed Darkest Africa in a balloon, descended to the centre of the earth, drifted in the South Atlantic, dying of thirst, and tasted—oh rapture! It always sent me indoors for a drink—the fresh waters of the Amazon." William Golding, "Astronaut by Gaslight," in *The Hot Gates, and Other Occasional Pieces* (New York: Harcourt, Brace, and World, 1965), 111.

p. 20, par. 1, This quotation comes from Golding's essay "On the Crest of the Wave," in which he explains why he feels that the arts are a more important study than science: "Our humanity, our capacity for living together in a full and fruitful life, does not reside in knowing things for the sake of knowing them or even in the power to exploit our surroundings. At best these are hobbies and toys—adult toys and I for one would not be without them. Our humanity rests in the capacity to make value judgments, unscientific assessments, the power to decide that this is right, that wrong, this ugly, that beautiful, this just, that unjust. Yet these are precisely the questions which 'Science' is not qualified to answer with its measurements and analysis. They can be answered only by the methods of philosophy and the arts. We are confusing the immense power which the scientific method gives us with the all-important power to make the value judgments which are the purpose of human education." In *The Hot Gates*, 130.

p. 28, par. 1, During the invasion of Walcheren, when his rocket ship had no air support, Golding tells Jack I. Biles that he grinned to mask his fear: "I was so frightened that this grin got stuck on my face, and it went on all the morning. We got shot up and everything, everybody was throwing stuff in every direction, there were colossal bangs and cascades of water. . . . Then there came one moment when we were just about to do a real death-and-glory run, and I still couldn't get rid of my grin." Because of Golding's smiling face, the crew at first thought the situation could not be too bad; but then they thought that their captain enjoyed fighting. They never guessed that Golding grinned merely to boost the morale of his crew when it was ordered on a suicide mission. When the order was canceled, Golding suddenly realized that he was going to live and his grin "fell off. . . . It just collapsed." The astonished crew thought he was disappointed, saying, "Do you see that old b--- up there? When he learnt we weren't going in, he was disappointed!" *Talk: Conversations with William Golding* (New York: Harcourt, Brace, Jovanovich, 1970), 28–29.

p. 30, par. 1, One of Golding's after-school activities was running an archaeology society, which he did for fifteen years. For as long as Golding can remember, he had an interest in archaeology because he was "always interested in how things were made and why" (Biles, 91). He recalls that when he was about ten years old, he rode his bike to watch local amateur archaeologist Augustus Pitt-Rivers excavate at Silbury Hill, the largest man-made mound in Europe: "Already archaeologists were heroes of mine, for some curious reason or other" (Biles, 92). Golding writes that archaeology was a way to stimulate his active imagination: "I like to pick through the ashcans of the Iron Age and guess how life went on." Golding, "Digging for Pictures," in *The Hot Gates*, 66. Ann Golding shared her husband's enthusiasm for archaeology, and together they took their young children to excavations of ancient sites.

p. 30, par. 3 Golding's daughter feels that her mother was instrumental in her father's success as a writer because "she encouraged him. She let him write. Crucially, she didn't make it difficult for him to spend time writing. She made a life for herself [acting, serving on committees, teaching part-time, lobbying, and visiting friends]. More than that, with her he felt safe to acknowledge his own, potentially disastrous, humanity. In a modern phrase, her love was unconditional. And I believe she also helped to feed his imaginative life." Judy Carver, "Harbour and Voyage: The Marriage of Ann and Bill Golding," in *Living with a Writer*, edited by Dale Salwak (New York: Palgrave Macmillan, 2004), 51.

p. 32, par. 2, Golding recalls the same story during an interview with Jack I. Biles: "I was sitting one side of the fire and Ann was sitting the other, and I had just been reading a G---awful book . . . about boys on an island, the usual adventure story. It wasn't [Ballantyne's] *The Coral Island* or anything else. I remember saying to Ann, 'Oh, I'm so tired of this business. Wouldn't it be fun to write a book about boys on an island and see what really happens?' And she said, 'That's an awfully good idea. You do that.' So I got a piece of paper and started to work out the story, and then everything went on, just like that, and there was not strain beforehand" (Biles, 60).

p. 33, par. 1, For a full discussion of the publication history of *Lord of the Flies* and the changes made to Golding's original text, see Charles Monteith, "Strangers from Within," in *William Golding: The Man and his Books, A Tribute on his 75th Birthday*, ed. John Carey

(New York: Farrar, Straus, and Giroux, 1986), 57–63. See also Virginia Tiger, *William Golding: The Unmoved Target* (New York: Marion Boyars, 2003), 31–33.

p. 33, par. 1, Golding was so caught up in *Lord of the Flies* that he says that when he got to the place in the novel in which he planned to write about human beings' inner evil, he had a type of mystic experience—his writing got "out of hand" and he began "writing at his [the pig's head] dictation": "It was at this point of imaginative concentration that I found that the pig's head knew Simon was there. In fact the Pig's head delivered something very like a sermon to the boy; the pig's head spoke. I know because I heard it." Golding, "Fable," in *The Hot Gates*, 99, 98.

p. 39, par. 3, There were four essays in *The Hot Gates, and Other Occasional Pieces* about his year in America. "A Touch of Insomnia," set on a ship taking him to America, is a comical spoof of the British class system, while "Body and Soul" describes the exhausting nature of the lecture circuit in which Golding was engaged. In "The Glass Door," Golding depicts the charm of a southern American college where the students "know absolutely nothing at all" about "the realities of life in the world at large" (142). His ambivalence about teaching a course in creative writing even though he is a visiting professor is examined in "Gradus ad Parnassum."

Chapter 3

p. 67, par. 1, All quotations to the novel come from William Golding, *Lord of the Flies* (New York: Penguin Books, 1999). All further references to this novel will be cited in the text.

p. 78, par. 1, A number of critics have criticized Golding's use of the coda as a contrived, artificial ending. But Virginia Tiger maintains that the "coda, with its reversed point of view on events contradicting initially established expectations, is a narrative feature of some subtlety, and not a 'gimmick.'" *William Golding: The Unmoved Target* (New York: Marion Boyars, 2003), 36.

p. 87, par. 1, For more information on the influence of the Greek gods on Golding's *Lord of the Flies*, see James R. Baker, *William Golding: A Critical Study* (New York: St. Martin's Press, 1965), 14–15; Lawrence S. Friedman, *William Golding* (New York: Continuum, 1993), 27–31; and Bernard F. Dick, *William Golding*, rev. ed. (Boston: Twayne Publishers, 1987), 30–31.

p. 89, par. 2, For a full discussion of the symbolism of the conch, see Ian Gregor and Mark Kinkead-Weekes, eds., *William Golding: A Critical Study of the Novels*, rev. 3rd ed. (London: Faber and Faber, 2002), 3–7.

p. 96, par. 1, A number of critics have compared J. D. Salinger's *The Catcher in the Rye* with Golding's novel. See Francis E. Kearns, "Salinger and Golding: Conflict on the Campus," in William Nelson, ed., *William Golding's "Lord of the Flies": A Source Book* (New York: Odyssey Press, 1963), 148–155; and Edmund Fuller, "Behind the Vogue, a Rigorous Understanding," in Nelson, 143–145.

ad on the stake. It becomes the Lord of the Flies, say-
cy thinking the Beast was something you could hunt and
You knew, didn't you? I'm part of you?" (128). Simon then
sciousness. After he recovers he forces himself up the
to discover the nature of the "beast" and finds the dead
st, whom he releases. He then attempts to join the oth-
ll them about his discovery. Meanwhile, all the boys,
g Ralph and Piggy, are in Jack's camp enjoying the pig
d participating in the pig-killing dance. When Simon
into the camp during the dance, the boys beat him to
inking he is the beast. Alone in the woods next to the
g's head, Simon listens to the head on the stake. It
he Lord of the Flies, saying, "Fancy thinking the Beast
hing you could hunt and kill! . . . You knew, didn't you?
of you?" (128). Simon then loses consciousness. After he
he forces himself up the mountain to discover the nature
east" and finds the dead parachutist, whom he releases.
ttempts to join the others to tell them about his dis-
eanwhile, all the boys, including Ralph and Piggy, are
camp enjoying the pig feast and participating in the
ng dance. When Simon stumbles into the camp during the
e boys beat him to death, thinking he is the beast. Alone
ods next to the bloody pig's head, Simon listens to the
the stake. It becomes the Lord of the Flies, saying,
inking the Beast was something you could hunt and kill!
new, didn't you? I'm part of you?" (128). Simon then loses
ness. After he recovers he forces himself up the moun-
iscover the nature of the "beast" and finds the dead
st, whom he releases. He then attempts to join the oth-
ll them about his discovery. Meanwhile, all the boys,
g Ralph and Piggy, are in Jack's camp enjoying the pig
d participating in the pig-killing dance. When Simon
into the camp during the dance, the boys beat him to
inking he is the beast. Alone in the woods next to the
g's head, Simon listens to the head on the stake. It
he Lord of the Flies, saying, "Fancy thinking the Beast
hing you could hunt and kill! . . . You knew, didn't you?
of you?" (128). Simon then loses consciousness. After he
he forces himself up the mountain to discover the nature
east" and finds the dead parachutist, whom he releases.
ttempts to join the others to tell them about his dis-
eanwhile, all the boys, including Ralph and Piggy, are

Further Information

Further Reading

Bloom, Harold. *William Golding's "Lord of the Flies."* Broomall, PA: Chelsea House Publishers, 1996.

Carver, Judy. "Harbour and Voyage: The Marriage of Ann and Bill Golding." In *Living with a Writer*. ed. Dale Salwak. Houndsmills, UK: Palgrave Macmillan, 2004, 44–55.

Friedman, Lawrence S. *William Golding*. New York: Continuum, 1993.

Golding, William. *The Hot Gates, and Other Occasional Pieces*. New York: Harcourt, Brace & World, 1966.

———. *Lord of the Flies*. New York: Penguin Books, 1999.

———. *A Moving Target*. New York: Farrar, Straus & Giroux, 1982.

Gregor, Ian and Mark Kinkead-Weekes, eds. *William Golding: A Critical Study of the Novels*. Rev. 3rd ed. London: Faber and Faber, 2002.

McCarron, Kevin. *William Golding*. Tavistock, UK: Northcote House Publishers, 2006.

Reilly, Patrick. *"Lord of the Flies": Fathers and Sons*. New York: Twayne Publishers, 1992.

Swisher, Claire, ed. *Readings on "Lord of the Flies."* San Diego, CA: Greenhaven Press, 1997.

Tiger, Virginia. *William Golding: The Unmoved Target.* New York: Marion Boyars, 2003.

Websites

Educational Paperback Association
http://www.edupaperback.org/showauth.cfm?authid=92
Reviews Golding's life and works.

LiteraryHistory.com
http://www.literaryhistory.com/20thC/Golding.htm
Contains a list of links to scholarly articles on William Golding.

Nobelprize.org
http://nobel.se/literature/laureates/1983/
Contains biography, bibliography, Nobel lecture, Nobel banquet speech, and other resources.

William Golding Website
http://www.william-golding.co.uk/
Website of the Golding family. Includes biography, photographs, materials for teachers, and materials for students.

Bibliography

Primary Sources

Golding, William. "Astronaut by Gaslight." In Golding, *The Hot Gates*, 111–115.

———. "Billy the Kid." In Golding, *The Hot Gates*, 159–165.

———. "Body and Soul." In Golding, *The Hot Gates*, 145–151.

———. *The Brass Butterfly*. London: Faber and Faber, 1958.

———. "Clonk Clonk." In Golding, *The Scorpion God*, 68–115.

———. *Close Quarters*. New York: Farrar, Straus & Giroux, 1979.

———. "Crosses." In Golding, *The Hot Gates*, 21–30.

———. *Darkness Visible*. New York: Farrar, Straus & Giroux, 1979.

———. "Digging for Pictures," In Golding, *The Hot Gates*, 61–70.

———. *The Double Tongue*. London: Faber and Faber, 1995.

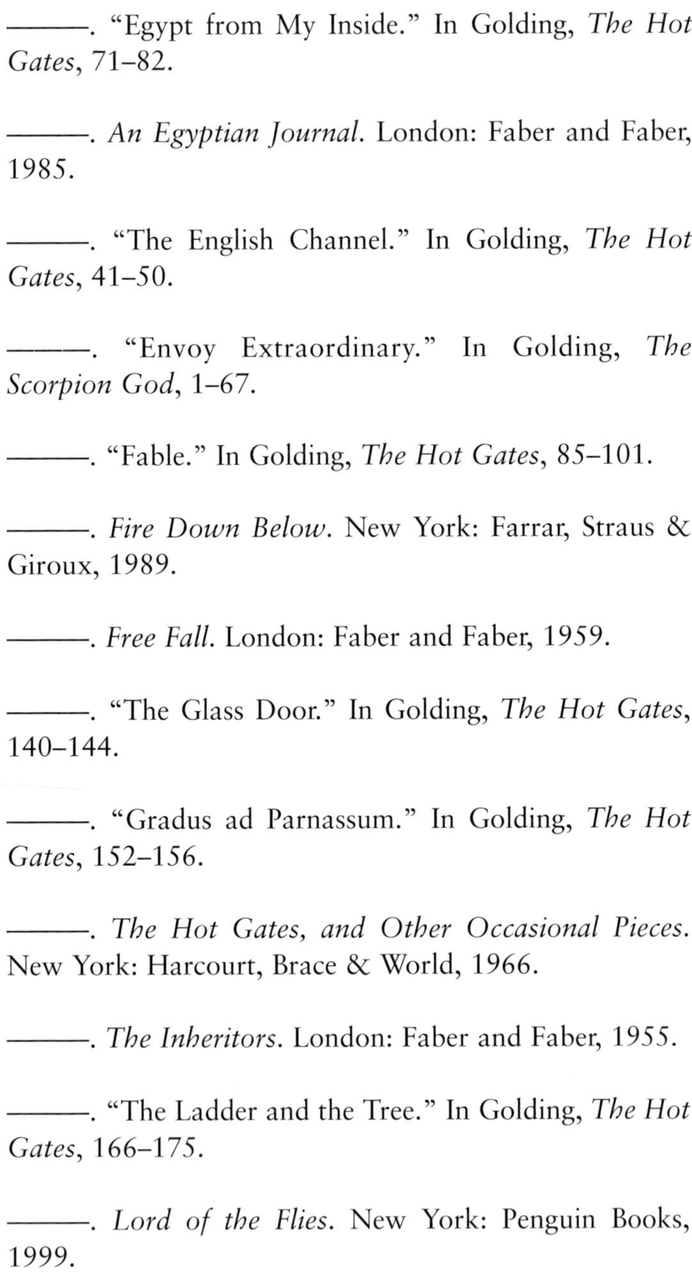

———. "Egypt from My Inside." In Golding, *The Hot Gates*, 71–82.

———. *An Egyptian Journal*. London: Faber and Faber, 1985.

———. "The English Channel." In Golding, *The Hot Gates*, 41–50.

———. "Envoy Extraordinary." In Golding, *The Scorpion God*, 1–67.

———. "Fable." In Golding, *The Hot Gates*, 85–101.

———. *Fire Down Below*. New York: Farrar, Straus & Giroux, 1989.

———. *Free Fall*. London: Faber and Faber, 1959.

———. "The Glass Door." In Golding, *The Hot Gates*, 140–144.

———. "Gradus ad Parnassum." In Golding, *The Hot Gates*, 152–156.

———. *The Hot Gates, and Other Occasional Pieces*. New York: Harcourt, Brace & World, 1966.

———. *The Inheritors*. London: Faber and Faber, 1955.

———. "The Ladder and the Tree." In Golding, *The Hot Gates*, 166–175.

———. *Lord of the Flies*. New York: Penguin Books, 1999.

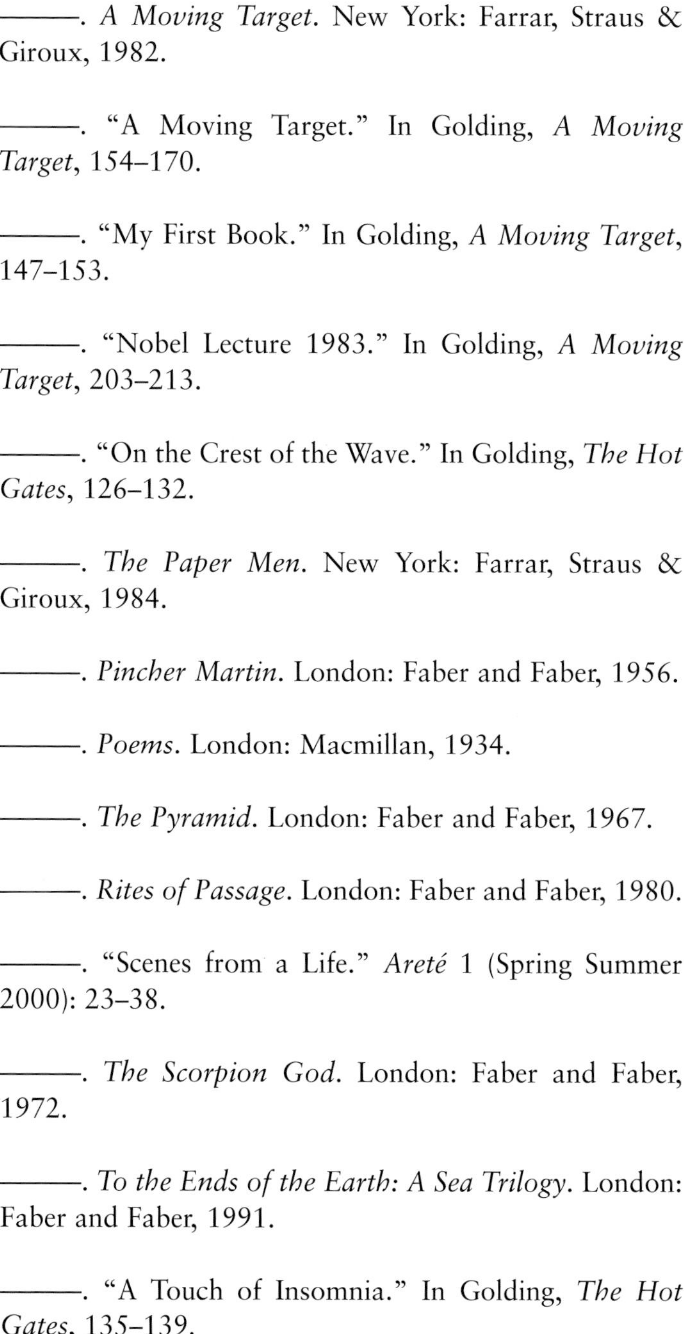

———. *A Moving Target*. New York: Farrar, Straus & Giroux, 1982.

———. "A Moving Target." In Golding, *A Moving Target*, 154–170.

———. "My First Book." In Golding, *A Moving Target*, 147–153.

———. "Nobel Lecture 1983." In Golding, *A Moving Target*, 203–213.

———. "On the Crest of the Wave." In Golding, *The Hot Gates*, 126–132.

———. *The Paper Men*. New York: Farrar, Straus & Giroux, 1984.

———. *Pincher Martin*. London: Faber and Faber, 1956.

———. *Poems*. London: Macmillan, 1934.

———. *The Pyramid*. London: Faber and Faber, 1967.

———. *Rites of Passage*. London: Faber and Faber, 1980.

———. "Scenes from a Life." *Areté* 1 (Spring Summer 2000): 23–38.

———. *The Scorpion God*. London: Faber and Faber, 1972.

———. *To the Ends of the Earth: A Sea Trilogy*. London: Faber and Faber, 1991.

———. "A Touch of Insomnia." In Golding, *The Hot Gates*, 135–139.

Secondary Sources

Allen, Walter. "New Novels." In Nelson, *William Golding's "Lord of the Flies,"* 3.

Baker, James R. *William Golding: A Critical Study*. New York: St. Martin's Press, 1965.

Barrett, Anthony. "Memories of Golding as a Schoolmaster." In Carey, *William Golding: The Man and his Books, A Tribute on his 75th Birthday*, 27–29.

Biles, Jack I. *Talk: Conversations with William Golding*. New York: Harcourt Brace Jovanovich, 1970.

Bloom, Harold. *William Golding's "Lord of the Flies."* Broomall, PA: Chelsea House Publishers, 1996.

Bowden, John. "From One Man's Meat, the Idea of Individual Responsibility." In Nelson, *William Golding's "Lord of the Flies,"* 54–55.

Boyd, S. J. *The Novels of William Golding*. Rev. ed. New York: Harvester Wheatsheaf, 1990.

Bufkin, E. C. "The Nobel Prize and the Paper Men: The Fixing of William Golding." *Georgia Review* 39 (1985): 55–65.

Callil, Carmen, and Colm Tóibín. "1954: *Lord of the Flies*." In *The Modern Library: The Two Hundred Best Novels in English Since 1950*. London: Picador, 1999, 66.

Carey, John. "William Golding talks [sic] to John Carey." In Carey, *William Golding: The Man and his Books, A Tribute on his 75th Birthday*, 171–189.

Carey, John, ed. *William Golding: The Man and his Books, A Tribute on his 75th Birthday*. New York: Farrar, Straus & Giroux, 1986.

Carver, Judy. "Harbour and Voyage: The Marriage of Ann and Bill Golding." In *Living with a Writer*. Edited by Dale Salwak. Houndsmills, UK: Palgrave Macmillan, 2004, 44–55.

———. "William Golding: A Biographical Sketch." In Gregor and Kinkead-Weekes, *William Golding*, 383–398.

Cox, C. B. "*Lord of the Flies*." In Nelson, *William Golding's "Lord of the Flies,"* 82–88.

Crompton, Donald W. *A View From the Spire: William Golding's Later Novels*. Edited and completed by Julia Briggs. Oxford: Blackwell, 1985.

Day, Martin S. *History of English Literature: 1837 to the Present*. New York: Doubleday, 1964.

Dick, Bernard F. *William Golding*. Rev. ed. Boston: Twayne Publishers, 1987.

Doering, Jonathan W. "The Fluctuations of William Golding's Critical Reputation." *Contemporary Review* 280.1636 (May 2002): 285–290.

Doyle, Robert P. *Banned Books: 2004 Resource Book*. Chicago, IL: American Library Association, 2004.

Drew, Philip. "Second Reading." In Nelson, *William Golding's "Lord of the Flies,"* 9–17.

Epstein, E. L. "Notes on *Lord of the Flies*." In Golding, *Lord of the Flies*, 188–192.

Everett, Barbara. "Golding's Pity." In Carey, *William Golding: The Man and his Books, A Tribute on his 75th Birthday*, 110–125.

Fowles, John. "Golding and 'Golding.'" In Carey, *William Golding: The Man and his Books, A Tribute on his 75th Birthday*, 146–156.

Fraser, Rebecca. *The Story of Britain: From the Romans to the Present: A Narrative History*. New York: W. W. Norton, 2003.

Friedman, Lawrence S. *William Golding*. New York: Continuum, 1993.

Fuller, Edmund. "Behind the Vogue, a Rigorous Understanding." In Nelson, *William Golding's "Lord of the Flies,"* 143–145.

Gindin, James. *Modern Novelists: William Golding*. New York: St. Martin's Press, 1988.

Gray, Paul. "A Prize as Good as Golding." *Time* (October 17, 1983): 97.

Green, Martin. "Distaste for the Contemporary." In Nelson, *William Golding's "Lord of the Flies,"* 75–82.

Green, Peter. "King Fix: Bill Golding in Greece." In Carey, *William Golding: The Man and his Book, A Tribute on his 75th Birthday*, 45–56.

Gregor, Ian and Mark Kinkead-Weekes, eds. *William Golding: A Critical Study of the Novels*. Rev. 3rd ed. London: Faber and Faber, 2002.

Halle, Louis J. "Small Savages." In Nelson, *William Golding's "Lord of the Flies,"* 5–6.

Heinlein, Robert A. *Tunnel in the Sky*. New York: Scribner, 1955.

Hewitt, Douglas. "New Novels." In Nelson, *William Golding's "Lord of the Flies,"* 4.

"Jack." Def. I.1.a. *The Oxford English Dictionary*. J. A. Simpson and E. S. C. Weiner, eds. Vol. 8. 2nd ed. Oxford: Clarendon Press, 1989, 162.

Johnston, Arnold. *Of Earth and Darkness: The Novels of William Golding*. Columbia: University of Missouri Press, 1980.

Jones, Ernest. *The Life and Work of Sigmund Freud*. Vol. 3. New York: Basic Books, 1957.

Kearns, Francis E. "Salinger and Golding: Conflict on the Campus." In Nelson, *William Golding's "Lord of the Flies,"* 148–155.

Keel, Paul, and W. L. Webb. "Patriotic Golding Claims Nobel Prize for England." *Guardian* (October 7, 1983): 1.

Kermode, Frank. "The Novels of William Golding." In Nelson, *William Golding's "Lord of the Flies,"* 107–120.

King, Stephen. *Cujo*. New York: Viking, 1981.

———. *Hearts in Atlantis*. New York: Scribner, 1999.

Loughead, Flora Haines. *Dictionary of Given Names with Their Origins and Meanings*. Glendale, CA: Arthur H. Clark Company, 1934.

McCarron, Kevin. *William Golding*. Tavistock, UK: Northcote House Publishers, 2006.

Medcalf, Stephen. "Bill and Mr [sic] Golding's Daimon." In Carey, *William Golding: The Man and his Books, A Tribute on his 75th Birthday*, 1986, 30–44.

———. *William Golding*. Edited by Ian Scott-Kilvert. Harlow, England: Longman Group, 1975.

———. "William Golding." *Independent* (June 21, 1993): 14.

Milton, John. *Paradise Lost*. Edited by Merritt Y. Hughes. New York: Odyssey Press, 1935.

Monteith, Charles. "Strangers from Within." In Carey, *William Golding: The Man and his Books, A Tribute on his 75th Birthday*, 57–63.

Moss, Peter. "Alec Albert Golding, 1876–1957." In Carey, *William Golding: The Man and his Books, A Tribute on his 75th Birthday*, 15–26.

Nelson, William, ed. *William Golding's "Lord of the Flies": A Source Book*. New York: Odyssey Press, 1963.

Oldsey, Bernard S., and Stanley Weintraub. *The Art of William Golding*. Bloomington: Indiana University Press, 1965.

Page, Norman, ed. *William Golding: Novels, 1954–1967*. Basingstoke and London: Macmillan, 1985.

Peck, John, and Martin Coyle. *A Brief History of English Literature*. Hampshire, GB: Palgrave, 2002.

Peter, John. "The Fables of William Golding." In Nelson, *William Golding's "Lord of the Flies,"* 21–34.

Pritchett, V. S. "Secret Parables." In Nelson, *William Golding's "Lord of the Flies,"* 35–39.

Reilly, Patrick. *"Lord of the Flies": Fathers and Sons.* New York: Twayne Publishers, 1992.

"Roger." Def. 1. *The Oxford English Dictionary*. J. A. Simpson and E. S. C. Weiner, eds. Vol. 14. 2nd ed. Oxford: Clarendon Press, 1989, 35.

Rosenfield, Claire. "Men of a Smaller Growth: A Psychological Analysis of William Golding's *Lord of the Flies*." In Nelson, *William Golding's "Lord of the Flies,"* 121–132.

Sinclair, Andrew. "William Golding's The Sea, The Sea." *Twentieth Century Literature*, 28.2 (Summer, 1982): 171–180.

Stern, James. "English Schoolboys in the Jungle." In Nelson, *William Golding's "Lord of the Flies,"* 6–7.

Tiger, Virginia. *William Golding: The Unmoved Target.* New York: Marion Boyars, 2003.

Time. "Lord of the Campus." In Nelson, *William Golding's "Lord of the Flies,"* 141–142.

Walters, Margaret. "Two Fabulists: Golding and Camus." In Nelson, *William Golding's "Lord of the Flies,"* 95–107.

Wickenden, Dan. "First Idyll, Then Nightmare." In Nelson, *William Golding's "Lord of the Flies,"* 8–9.

Index

Page numbers in **boldface** are illustrations, tables, and charts. Proper names of fictional characters are shown by (C).

About the Author

Raychel Haugrud Reiff, a Professor of English at the University of Wisconsin-Superior, has published seven books in Marshall Cavendish Benchmark's Writers and Their Works series, as well as numerous articles on literary topics. Her most recent book in this series is *Aldous Huxley: Brave New World*. She lives in Superior, Wisconsin.